Writing 34

EDWARD DORN

THE COLLECTED POEMS
1956–1974

Four Seasons Foundation
Bolinas · California

Second printing, with revisions

Book design and composition by Zoe Brown

Library of Congress Cataloging in Publication Data

Dorn, Edward.
    Collected poems, 1956-1974.

    (Writing ; 34)
    . Includes index.
PS3507.073277A17 1975   811'.5'4   74-27227
ISBN 0-87704-030-3
ISBN 0-87704-029-X pbk.

The Writing Series is edited by Donald Allen, published by the Four Seasons Foundation, and distributed by Book People, 2940 Seventh Street, Berkeley, California 94710.

PREFACE

This collection contains my work of the past 18 years with the exception, most notably, of the dramatic narrative *Gunslinger*, which was evoked on another scale. As with any anatomy there are structures in this body to which I can no longer assign a use and whose functions are hidden. Throughout this period I have published through persons, and except for two cases not represented here, not with houses. I have stayed with that care because it is accurate and important. Important equally for those who have published me. From near the beginning I have known my work to be theoretical in nature and poetic by virtue of its inherent tone. My true readers have known exactly what I have assumed. I am privileged to take this occasion to thank you for that exactitude, and to acknowledge the pleasure of such a relationship.

Edward Dorn

San Francisco,
September, 1974

ACKNOWLEDGEMENTS

The Newly Fallen. New York: Totem Press in association with The Paterson Society, 1961. LeRoi Jones and Elsa Dorfman.
Hands Up! New York: Totem Press in association with Corinth Books, 1964. LeRoi Jones and Ted Wilentz.
From Gloucester Out. London: Matrix Press, 1964. Tom Raworth.
Geography. London: Fulcrum Press, 1965. Stuart Montgomery.
The North Atlantic Turbine. London: Fulcrum Press, 1967. Stuart Montgomery.
Twenty-four Love Poems. West Newbury: Frontier Press, 1969. Harvey Brown.
Songs, Set Two. West Newbury: Frontier Press, 1970. Harvey Brown.

UNCOLLECTED

"The World Box-score." *Thrice, Slice,* Brightlingsea, 1966. *El Corno Emplumado* 26, Mexico City, 1968. *Free Poems,* Artists' Workshop, Detroit, 1968.
"The Cosmology of Finding Your Place." Presented April 10, 1969 at the United Campus Christian Fellowship Benefit Reading for the Draft Resisters League, Lawrence.
"The Kultchural Exchange." *Toothpick, Lisbon and the Orcas Islands,* May 1971, Seattle.
"The Poet Lets His Tongue Hang Down." *Paris Review* XIV, 55 (Fall 1972); *Vort* I (Fall 1972); *The Boston Phoenix,* 7 November 1972.
"The History of Futures." *The World,* Spring 1973.
"The Octopus Thinks With Its Arms." ZI Broadside, Summer 1973; *Contemporary Literature* XV, 3, Madison.

CONTENTS

THE COLLECTED POEMS

THE RICK OF GREEN WOOD

In the woodyard were green and dry
woods fanning out, behind
                        a valley below
a pleasure for the eye to go.

Woodpile by the buzzsaw. I heard
the woodsman down in the thicket. I don't
want a rick of green wood, I told him
I want cherry or alder or something strong
and thin, or thick if dry, but I don't
want the green wood, my wife would die

Her back is slender
and the wood I get must not
bend her too much through the day.

Aye, the wood is some green
and some dry, the cherry thin of bark
cut in July.

My name is Burlingame
said the woodcutter.
My name is Dorn, I said.
I buzz on Friday if the weather cools
said Burlingame, enough of names.

       Out of the thicket my daughter was walking
singing—
           backtracking the horse hoof
gone in earlier this morning, the woodcutter's horse
pulling the alder, the fir, the hemlock
above the valley
                 in the november

air, in the world, that was getting colder
as we stood there in the woodyard talking
pleasantly, of the green wood and the dry.

[1956]

VAQUERO

The cowboy stands beneath
a brick-orange moon. The top
of his oblong head is blue, the sheath
of his hips
is too.

In the dark brown night
your delicate cowboy stands quite still.
His plain hands are crossed.
His wrists are embossed white.

In the background night is a house,
has a blue chimney top,
Yi Yi, the cowboy's eyes
are blue. The top of the sky
is too.

THE HIDE OF MY MOTHER

1
My mother, who has a hide
on several occasions remarked what

4

a nice rug or robe
my young kids would make,

Would we send them to her?
When we had them butchered?

It was certainly a hoo ha ha
from me
and a ho ho
from my wife: and I would amusedly say
to conceal the fist in my heart
which one? the black?

or the grey
& white?

And she would smile, exposing the carnival
in her head

What's the difference, after they're dead?

Can you imagine asking a poet that?
Perhaps I should tell her about my pet rat.

2
My mother remarked
that in Illinois

little boys sell holly
from door to door,

and *here,* she would say
they grow all over the mountains
what if I took a holly tree back
there? would it grow?
No. I said.

3
Once my mother
was making dinner

and my cats were on the floor.

Why do they whine like that?
she asked,

why don't we throw them all out the door?
why don't you feed them I ventured?

She said she wasn't indentured.

Can you imagine telling a poet that?
Later she fed them my pet rat.

4
One day my son
found a parakeet in the bush
brought it to the house
carrying the little blue thing by the tail.

My mother said why, isn't it pretty,
I wonder if it would make the trip home
to Illinois. Oh, I said, we'll have to find its owner

you don't want to pull a boner
like that.

5
Tho winter's at term
it still gets cold

in the evening.
My pets are warm

because I have set a fire.

My mother is arranging some ferns
and young trees, a little too big

she found in the mountains.
A jig, of a sort must be going

on in her head. It is raining
outside. Do you think I can get the copper legs

of that stool in the box
or is it too wide? With some of those

pretty rocks I saw on the beach, would you,
she was saying to my little boy,

like to go home to Illinois with grandmother?

He was saying from inside the box enclosure,
he wasn't sure he

wanted to leave his mother.

6
For a point of etiquette,
when I observed she was digging
the neighbor's English privet,

I said, it grows in abundance here.

As a matter of fact, she had it,
I thought I saw a rabbit,
that's why I came over here.

I said, a plant like that might grow anywhere.

Well now, I suppose you are right
back home our elms have the blight
but the land is flat there
so many mountains hereabouts

Yes, I allowed, it must help the sprouts . . .

Well now, there's more rain here
than we have in Illinois in an entire year
wouldn't you think tho it would grow there?

I said, what about a privet hedge from . . .

You remember the peonies on grandfather's grave
well someone took them they were gone
the last Memorial Day I was there

. . . From Hudson's Bay to the Gulf of Carpentaria.
Do you think it would stay?

Oh I love plants but where I am the weather
drives the birds away.

7
As for the hides of other people,
My wife told her

of how the junkman's
woman had been so good to us

a truss as it were, had kept the children
when it was a hardship

the condition had been foul, sleet,
masses of air, a raw affair,

dumped out of the Yukon upon
us, roving bands of weather

sliding across British Columbia
a kind of dementia

of the days, frozen water pipes
and the wringer on the washing machine

busted, no coal.
Our house split in two like Pakistan.

The graciousness
of the woman of the junkman

she said. Now what do you think
we should do? forget it? some doughnuts?
a cake?

"Why, I don't know what I would do" –
my mother was alluding

to a possible misfortune of her own.

8
As for the thick of it,
really, my mother
never knew about the world.

I mean even that there was one,
or more.

Whorled, like a univalve shell
into herself,

early to bed, nothing
in her head, here and there

Michigan one time,   Ohio

another. Led a life
like a novel, who hasn't?

As for Sociology:
garbage cans were what she dumped
the remains of supper in,

dirty newspapers, if blowing
in the street, somebody probably

dropped them there.

Nobody told her about the damned
or martyrdom. She's 47

so that, at least, isn't an emergency.

Had a chance to go to Arizona once
and weighed the ins and outs

to the nearest ounce:
didn't go. She was always slow.

Incidently, for her the air
was Red one time:

tail end of a dust storm
somehow battered up from Kansas.

[1957]

ARE THEY DANCING

There is a sad carnival up the valley
The willows flow it seems on trellises of music
Everyone is there today, everyone I love.

There is a mad mad fiesta along the river
Thrilling ladies sing in my ear, where
Are your friends, lost? They were to come

And banjoes were to accompany us all
And our feet were to go continually
The sound of laughter was to flow over the water

What was to have been, is something else
I am afraid. Only a letter from New Mexico
And another from a mountain by Pocatello,

I wonder, what instruments are playing
And whose eyes are straying over the mountain
Over the desert
And are they dancing: or gazing at the earth.

THE AIR OF JUNE SINGS

Quietly and while at rest on the trim grass I have gazed,
admonished myself for having never been here
at the grave-side and read the names of my Time Wanderers.
And now, the light noise of the children at play on the inscribed stone

jars my ear and they whisper and laugh covering their mouths. "My
    Darling"
my daughter reads, some of the markers
reflect such lightness to her reading eyes, yea, as I rove
among these polished and lime blocks I am moved to tears and I hear
the depth in "Darling, we love thee," and as in "Safe in Heaven."

I am going off to heaven and I won't see you anymore. I am
going back into the country and I won't be here anymore. I am
going to die in 1937. But where did you die my Wanderer?
You, under the grave-grass, with the tin standard whereat
I look, and try to read the blurred ink. I cannot believe
you were slighted knowing what I do of cost and evil
yet tin is less than granite. Those who buried you should have known
a 6 inch square of sandstone, flush with the earth
is more proper for the gone than blurred and faded flags.

Than the blurred and faded flags I am walking with in the graveyard.

Across the road in the strawberry field two children are stealing
their supper fruit, abreast in the rows, in the fields of the overlord,
Miller his authentic name, and I see that name represented here,
there is that social side of burial too, long residence,
and the weight of the established local dead. My eyes avoid
the largest stone, larger than the common large, Goodpole Matthews,
Pioneer, and that pioneer sticks in me like a wormed black cherry
in my throat, No Date, nothing but that zeal, that trekking
and Business, that presumption in a sacred place, where children
are buried, and where peace, as it is in the fields and the country
should reign. A wagon wheel is buried there. Lead me away

to the small quiet stones of the unpreposterous dead and leave
me my tears for Darling we love thee, for Budded on earth and
     blossomed
in heaven, where the fieldbirds sing in the fence rows,
and there is possibility, where there are not the loneliest of all.

Oh, the stones not yet cut.

                                                        [1958]

WHEN THE FAIRIES

When the fairies come back to Santa Fe
they sit in dark caverns called taverns
and eat nervously picking at their food.

When they come back to Santa Fe
they gesticulate nervously and it's London
is meant.

When you pass their tables you see
their fingers flying off from Santa Fe
to Dakar or somewhere very far
away where neither you nor they
have ever been.

Still, they are nervous and pick at their food.

When the fairies fly back to Santa Fe
coming in on their smelly little wings
they gesticulate and Paris is meant
and they play games like guess what
book is meant,

and what color

and order drinks no one can mix.

They are a witchy bunch
and very inarticulate and late
in the day they order a lunch no one can assemble,

which they attack nervously
guessing what color —
where Copenhagen is meant

guessing what color and raiment.

[1959]

GERANIUM

I know that peace is soon coming, and love of common object,
and of woman and all the natural things I groom, in my mind, of
faint rememberable patterns, the great geography of my lunacy.

I go on my way frowning at novelty, wishing I were closer to home
than I am. And this is the last bus stop before Burlington,
that pea-center, which is my home, but not the home of my mind.
That asylum I carry in my insane squint, where beyond
the window a curious woman in the station door
has a red bandana on her head, and tinkling things hand themselves
to the wind that gathers about her skirts. In the rich manner of her kind
she waits for the bus to stop. Lo, a handsome woman.

Now, my sense decays, she is the flat regularity, the brick
of the station wall, is the red Geranium of my last Washington stop.
Is my object no shoes brought from india
can make exotic, nor hardly be made antic would she astride
a motorcycle (forsake materials and we shall survive together)
nor be purchased by the lust of schedule.

13

No,

on her feet therefore, are the silences of nothing. And leather
leggings adorn her limbs, on her arms are the garlands of ferns
come from a raining raining forest and dripping lapidary's dust.
She is a common thief of fauna and locale (in her eyes
are the small sticks of slender land-bridges) a porter
standing near would carry her bundle, which is scarlet too,

as a geranium and cherishable common that I worship and that I sing
ploddingly, and out of tune as she, were she less the lapwing
as she my pale sojourner, is.

THE SPARROW SKY

Through the window
on the branch
against the evening winter sky
a blue bird
rests on the branch
and a natural shaking will take
its place it flew off
departing the recoil
slight and brief to me
who am that branch standing.

Will be
a form of breast and nodding head
an arrival from the vast mid-west,
where I was on a flat nearly black plain
where evening has
the same color,
empty as that branch filled
with the summer dense locust
and silent under a burden of months
when summer waved away,
a slight recoil,
and snow began to come.

Where sparrows are
the only lifting in the winter
along sentinel fences, among
the rows of stubbles and thin lights
of small towns

Where the light
and all such branches of whipping hickory
start my sadness not violently,
as a yearning to be gone,
but softly, as the remote pleasure of the solstice.

Purple *is* fashionable twice
at this season (of lifting our heads)
—it is November, and I am with
the shadow of a bird
gone elsewhere now like a shield
across my own hollowed self
a red barn
where the hayropes hang like webs
and the starving sparrows sit
in the lofts
not chirping
for the new wings coming
up to roost.

3 FARM POEMS

1. THE WAR

And my frail legs
were filled with needles of fright
upstairs under the crazy quilt
December 7, 1941,
that same place, an isolated farm
Eastern Illinois, I overheard it later
because on Sunday it was sermons all day
messages of what
I first listened to waiting for the Shadow
only the Shadow knows heh heh heh
and at night sitting like a dream she was
near the bedroom, who went once to my mother
and said I had rheumatic fever, rumors
of fever in the sunny days of summer
through corn fields running
the rich yellow dusty pollen tassels
striking my face like the gold we barely
heard of, it was not
our harvest, it was not
our field, it was not gold fever.

2. THE TOUCH

Returning to the first nights
spent in open dream, a desolate fiesta
to encounter
a woman past all desire
that false setting so far gone—a fragment
like the bark of a dog in the road, returns
an anger of silence or the war
on the horizon,
what is called "false water."

3. GOODBYE TO THE ILLINOIS

Where out of the black dirt
screens are put up, shocks
men come blindly to harvest
and eat large meals in the larger houses
and the rest of the year you sit in a small house not knowing
how many rooms you want, not guessing
how many there are
of heat giving rise to plants of illusion
soft winds blowing yellow pollen across the rows
and in seclusion babies are born
in spring, where oh but in winter
the black vanes of elders everywhere
or walnut along the river break the sky
a meaningless map, a meaningless riddle
of what in simpler life would say was lost
in space, rising as debris in tornadoes,
but were really chaffs
of hay in July, oh mother
I remember your year-long stare
across plowed flat prairielands.

THE OPEN ROAD

The man stood
in his house
and thought to himself
the fence fell down—
mad elements to be scrutinized.

What a grey morning
it is it is

17

unusual after a night
where the bright moon
shone—that was fivethirty
now it is six

what a grey morning I am.
The man stood
    in his room, a lock
of his hair fell
over his fair temple
and his thought
aptly changed now

from his own temple
wherein he is King
to the moon, gone

no longer orange in the dawn
sky but a thing
elsewhere rising, thus
the poet

of that cosmos
knows it is
in small phenomena
as these

he will increase the
daily imagery
and bring within the ease
of all, the powers anciently
attributed and forthcoming
from the muse, those women
who held another temple,

whose existence lately
taken as a ruse
such lordly powers
to be more equitably
divided and strewn

abroad,
enlightening these new walking
palaces shining into every roofed
structure where sits a man

mouseling bravely lording
it on his own
in this newest of all empires

an imperialism that will
live to surpass in heat Africa's

outstretched limbs
and beat against
those seductive shores where whole
nations nightly
whore for mines
and rivers overhung as
the thoughts of all

those particles of men
who are the outriders of golden dreams
and who wake to a grey morning
finding themselves
that their homey

delvings gleam
only with cotton batting lions
trotting no more breathlessly
than they

across paper horizons
yet that real lion NAR
laughs quietly not quite satisfied
at the month's receipts
from Katanga.

The man challenges his anger
with the coolest philosophy
dealing with the rumble

of afterthoughts
aluminum pots and pans
copper bottoms,
            or a cheerfulness
constituting the recollection
of old gang fights—
a wayward memory of active men

or admiring the bum
for its abandonment to despair
but for his own ego, he
excuses it;
as something which he *has*
if nothing else,
            thus he is
enthusiastic for the opposite of despair

Which to a hopeful man is also
a real lion drowsing
from too full a meal
or it is the wheel of fortune rolling
forward over the bodies
of those who were bent in labor.

Of which it is said this force
we can thank for making we coarse ones
from the multitudes
poets

for the earth, this pear,
as domicile has been shaken loose
has been taken
as more impermanent
than any apartment
or house on a shady street
or any interior thing, covered
if possible, but a shelter
to hide under, furnished by a grand
commonplace—

This is just to say
I have eaten
the plums
that were in
the icebox

THE SONG

So light no one noticed
so lightly she could not care
or her deep dark eyes would have turned
saw I surmised in my fear
her walk was troubled for she tried
my eyes with her grace,
her secret wave
with her fingers
had luck willed,
been real, been an ending to a life
of small tears.

            Thus days go by
and I stand knowing her hair
in my mind as a dark cloud, its presence
straying over the rim of a volcano
of desire, and I take something
so closed as a book
into the world where she is.

Our love,
Like a difficult memory lives and revisits
in certain dreams at night
or during days when I am tired
of the blight of the poorly tuned sounds

of where I am, times
which make me beholden to please
the motions of those I talk with
eat with sleep with plead with
need. Concerning love
the first trace that slips to the ground
leaving all space above, into which one can enter
was mother? Lespuge is a figure
of dreamed wholeness, the form
is born of that desire
the whole swelling difficulty.

SOUSA

Great brass bell of austerity
and the ghosts of old picnickers
ambling under the box elder, when the sobriety
was the drunkenness. John,

you child, there is no silence
you can't decapitate
and on forgotten places (the octagonal
stand, Windsor, Illinois, the only May Day
of my mind) the fresh breeze
and the summer dresses of girls once blew
but do not now. They blow now at the backs
of our ears John,
under the piñon,
that foreign plant with arrogant southern smell.
I yearn for the box elder and its beautiful
bug, the red striped and black plated—
your specific insect, in the Sunday after noon.

Oh restore my northern madness
which no one values anymore and shun
its uses, give them back their darkened instinct
(which I value no more) we are
dedicated to madness that's why I love you
Sousa, you semper fidelis maniac.

And the sweep
of your american arms
bring a single banging street in Nebraska
home, and your shock
when a trillion broads smile at you
their shocking laughter can be heard long after
the picknickers have gone home.

March us home through the spring rain
the belief, the relief
of sunday occasion.

Your soft high flute and brass
remind me of a lost celebration I can't
quite remember,
in which I volunteered as conqueror:
the silence now stretches me
into sadness.

Come back into the street bells
and tin soldiers.

      • •

But there are no drums
no drums, loudness,
no poinsettia shirts,
there is no warning, you won't recognize anyone.

Children and men in every way
milling, gathering daily (those vacant eyes)
the bread lines of the deprived are here
Los Alamos, 1960, not Salinas
not Stockton.

Thus when mouths are opened,
waves of poison rain will fall, butterflies
do not fly up from any mouth in this place.

•   •

Let me go away,
shouting alone, laughing
to the air, Sousa be here
when the leaves wear
a blank radio green, for honoring.

Dwell again in the hinterland
and take your phone,
play to the lovely eyed people in the field
on the hillside.

Hopeful, and kind
merrily and possible
(as my friend said, "Why can't it be
like this all the time?"
her arms spread out before her).

•   •

John Sousa you can't now
amuse a nation with colored drums
even with cymbals, their ears
have lifted the chalice of explosion
a glass of straight malice, and
we wander in Random in the alleys
of their longfaced towns taking
from their sickly mandibles handbills
summoning our joint spirits.

I sing Sousa.

The desire to disintegrate the Earth
is eccentric,
And away from centre
nothing more nor sizeable
nor science

nor ennobling
no purity, no endeavor
toward human grace.

• •

We were
on a prominence though
so lovely to the eye eyes
of birds only caught
all the differences
of each house filled hill.

And from the window a spire
of poplar, windows
and brown pater earth buildings.

My eye on the circling bird
my mind lost in the rainy hemlocks of Washington
the body displaced, let it
wander all the way to Random and dwell
in those damp groves
where stand the friends
I love and left: behind me
slumbering under the dark morning sky

are my few friends.

Please
cut wood to warm them
and stalk never appearing animals
to warm them,
I hope they are warm tonight—
bring salmonberries
even pumpkinseed.

Sousa,
it can never be
as my friend said
"Why can't it be like this all the time?"
Her arms spread out before her

25

gauging the alarm,
(with that entablature)
and the triumph of a march
in which no one
is injured.

THE TOP LIST

They have a list of 10
plus 500 minor ones
they make plans & leave in the night
and have the money to get there
though few
if any
        are privately wealthy.
A truck pulled up in the night.
They got out, their eyes glowed like amber
amber as old as the hills they sped across.
What crime is not counter-crime?
What men are not bossed?
When will they again come
to strange shores to gratify their
national memories?
Not even helpless abominable criminals
can escape them—
I am glad I am not famous,
this time would be bad for that.
Still we all have cause for terror.

THE PRISONER OF BELLEFONTE (PA)

Was unknown to me.
And was nothing to me.
I shut my eyes
    as he went to the electric chair, I slept
perhaps on a cool Monday night.
Some men have cast the thought that we are
pebbles shifting on the beaches
of the world where the influences of tides
touch us all, but is that wise?—
for poets least, in whose feeling rides
more power than in that allegory.

            But I opened my eyes in the morning
as he did not, he'd changed,
                    because he died,
at a place called shippingport, where
for all we know Pluto may still come
to surface.
The straps
on his sagging head with its eyes turned
finally up,
the shackles on his cooked wrists,
and the lead helmet given the cops
by heaven and Sir James Jeans.

And outside, the careful transformer
reducing what Cleveland Thompson was not
to be allowed to have too much of.
    That precious stuff, World
has more useful purposes, oh
for moving the pebbles on the beach.

I wish they hadn't
            because I read
that he cried, and didn't want to go,
hung back, and was carried screaming . . .

it is those ugly thrills in the spine
that come when the meeting with death is arranged,
that no man can stand.

It is grand having not heard him,
over the radio,
because someone sings The End of a Love Affair,
and they say the people of the community
got the woman he raped
a job in a factory,
like Darwin's Tierra del Fuegoan
they took her back to make a go for them.

LIKE A MESSAGE ON SUNDAY

Sits
    the forlorn plumber
by the river
with his daughter
    staring at the water
then, at her
his daughter closely.

Once World, he came
to our house to fix the stove
                and couldn't
    oh, we were arrogant and talked
about him in the next room, doesn't
a man know what he is doing?

Can't it be done right,
        World of iron thorns.
Now they sit by the meagre river
by the water . . . stare

into that plumber
so that I can see a daughter in the water
she thin and silent,
he, wearing a baseball cap
    in a celebrating town this summer season
may they live on

on, may their failure be kindly, and come
in small unnoticeable pieces.

OUR CAMP

was pitched on a slope
where all herbs thrived
but was beleaguered
by little determined men
for the most part we never knew
at all.

                There were no beginnings
no initial apple,
no man or woman, as those entities
are understood by all.

  The slight stories of explanation
were never meant to be remembered, they are
as change, counted, and then pocketed:

                            0 was one
of their determining inventions
zero, for an empty class, a symbol for nothing,
endowed the void.
The counting board became carryable

into our camp,
Zeno of Elea, our enemy, said—
"But what has been said once, can always be repeated"
and this was not a new idea
even in his time.

  Into our camp came music, and some
danced, there was the love of
a warm hand on our lives, but centuries later someone
pointed out the nail grows faster
on the hand that's used, be it left or right.
Measures were so arrogant . . .
One nation is corrupt as the others
classically are, classic
is that which has the durability of stone
and hangs in our stomachs until
the day of removal comes.

THE ARGUMENT IS

That worn clothes look
as nice
on the children down the road
playing and running in the afternoon
that these clothes are used,
these castoffs
we are castoff from—all the elegant
running little retailers, here
and in the next crossroads town.

    But the dress one little girl
blithely wore, unaware
an argument as to the ways of society

was going on around her—
a long yellow dress
flowers
pulled in at the waist, nearly
sweeping the ground.

Oh, they are now pagan
these old castoffs,
but as rationale one sees the grime
sees the face broken in dark lines of consumption.

Of wearing secretly a burden,
costumes fitting as casually as though
they were stolen,
from the wealth
of the nation.

A COUNTRY SONG

"And I pluck'd a hollow reed,
And I made a rural pen"

BLAKE

1
Thru the window
Cherry tree limbs

Thru the country
The air climbs

Over the fields
And along the road

The country woman
Comes to her abode

Over a letter
Her eye wanders

From a sister
Who wonders

How she is there
On the farm

In the country air.

2
Thru the window
The cherry branch

Against the bright sky
I in this room chance

To set my head
Against the wall

Awaiting the woman
Her entering footfall

On the porch, saying—
Sit down

And stay awhile
Here's a letter from town

And did you see
The daffodils

Spring, is coming early.

3
Thru the window
The cherry broods

—We've come here, sat
We haven't stood

Nor waited long
The quiet is amazing

And the stove fire
Very blazing

It must be wild
To get drunk on the country

In the cold burning air
When the orchard is empty

When winter stares with sloe eye
Thru bright windows

And Spring, is coming early.

4
Thru the window
The man stood

Against a rake
He broods

By a burning bush
He thinks of the ground

And the garden
To be grown

And the harvest
To be gathered

In the fall.
A winter-time piece tethered

In his eye
Ideas of the land

Under a cold blue sky.

5
Thru the windows
The man's hair

Shines white his bright
Bush dies in the fair

Wind, and he throws
The remaining sticks

On the fire then looks
Toward the house and picks

Up the tools
The children run

To greet him, they enter
The house with the sun

Going down under the tree
What a wild thing

To be in the country.

6
Thru the door
They come

Thru the day
They have gone

As the world turned
Around

He cleared the
Beckoning ground

Now the yellow strings
Of dusk hang in the air

They read the letter
From the sister,

Then in front of the fire
We talk of Spring

An obscure slight offering.

PRAYERS FOR THE PEOPLE OF THE WORLD

They were an exercise the ages go through
smiling in the church one time
banging and blowing in the street another
where brother is a state very often of glue
coming apart in the heat
of British Guiana where
the drainage and open canals
make difficult the protection of the lower classes
who have lands and moneys, food and shelter
in the great escrow called Never

Did America say give me your poor?
Yes for poor is the vitamin not stored
it goes out in the urine of all endeavor.
So Poor came in long black flea coats
and bulgarian hats
spies and bombers
and she made five rich while flies covered the rest
who were suppressed or murdered
or out-bred their own demise.

AND THUS

We like Agamemnon
the most notorious
cuckold the world has known
have mutilated emotions.
Don't pity us, nor be pleased
with us.
                    The bulwark of trifles
against which we throw ourselves
looms larger, granted
than the shade thrown
by the towering white scarps of
Greenland tonight, and is noisier
than the North Sea where spikes of sea
grow like white flowers.
The myths of the netherlands were not lost
they were thrown too belligerently into the wind.

Our days
recur to how
we made the world, how we desired
to live long rather than quickly,
but when our eyes seek those hills
too late, from which the sun is taking
away its power, a landsman turns
thinking a friend may come across
the long horizon to greet him, but it is only
the dust walking,
                    which rises up
around us, around too
the yellow waterless chamiso far south.

THERE WAS A CHANGE

the weather broke up
like rocks, landslides
in the sky's terrain
all falling down
to where a palisade of white
now holds the horizon.

On the mountains
which are an appellation
of blood called sangre
            the white spears
of slopes cut down
into the lower altitudes

a firm thrust, a decision
at this height,
and for those things.

            The apricot
is the first to bloom
then comes the apple.
Already the blossom
            of the apricot
has gone,
            the clouds
are drifting up on the breeze
their darkening undersides
                        the ballast
of a change.

And all our friends will return
crossing the dry frontier river
traveling north.

HI   a change in the weather.
HI   a friend's return.

IF IT SHOULD EVER COME

And we are all there together
time will wave as willows do
and adios will be truly, yes,

    laughing at what is forgotten
and talking of what's new
admiring the roses you brought.
How sad.

You didn't know you were at the end
thought it was your bright pear
the earth, yes

another affair to have been kept
and gazed back on
when you had slept
to have been stored
as a squirrel will a nut, and half
forgotten,
there were so many, many
from the newly fallen.

THE DEER'S EYE THE HUNTER'S NOSE

Steel moon hooves
bang the hard grey earth.
flash.
by their
       clatter flown
against the froze red barnwalls
the ruts

break and shatter off barndoors
the acoustic
cold breaks on
       the ear of the acaudate hunter
a year of dead beetles . . .
upon us the mountain
affronting hills.
Idaho rocks drop
inside an old mine where deer's
eyes wind the light into
yellow balls
back of darkness—away
down under the plaid hat hunter's tread
who spreads a plaid tongue
on his lip, guessing
with his quick alcoholic glance—
there is no scent
in the nose of him
just snot
              and we in a shack
hear his shot, vowing
to return the fire
we have a howitzer
for such a siege—
but guess the horse runs, sparking eye
streaming nostrils, drops
gleaming froze turds
which, hitting the ground rattle
enormous grapeshot down the hill.
flash.
the deer eye opens in the mind
on the acoustics of the hunt—is it
the run of the horse is it
the blunt diarrhea of the gun
is it the rage of the horse.

WAGON WHEELS

Hands on a surcingle
hands on a hackamore
demanding because they paid
their money
to be like the first blackamoor
      in these parts
strange cowboys live
in ranch style houses.

Say one of them sees
his horse every day or so
like that,
but another wants the west wide
like that, refusing
population, a monster to him.

Yet exhausted it still moves
across "the precious uncluttered
land" as its will takes it
plastic boats behind.

THE SEA CORNER, OF THE EYE

He haunted the inland
the sea was
            a dust storm, dust
he thought,

he never thought of borders nor had to
the precious thoughts of poets

were pushing against those
as he rode

    just past Sundance
    having come from

Bell Fourche,

on his throbbing black Norton.

A new day had dawned.
A tear is now his merciless eye
in the wind.

But not known to him
                anymore
than the beryllium mine off
in the rushing hills
where Calamity Jane yielded once
a meat axe
a meat axe in the low disc

Of the dark sun and whose ache
was the heart of the dispossessed
as his mind
            could not grasp
the spreading contours
of his inland either.

What shall we do?
As we lie here he speeds on and his direction
may never bend
may like a windborn seed
obscure space.

TRAIL CREEK, AUG. 11,
THE REASON OF HIGHER POWERS

Sage smoke
has a bad effect on the nose
the head aches
from its fullness, running
along the edge of the flaming grass
the lungs refuse to take it.

The rain clouds promise
to finish our work, over
the mountain top clouds rush
but yield nothing.

The southern boy with Alaska
sewn to his shirt sleeve says
there wasn't nothing to do there—
I finally went to the PX and bought
me a gun.

The idle mind is a receptacle
for all casual dissatisfaction
and loitering. The breeze is
still hot from the fire as we wait.

Below the silver water tank
at the brink of the fire line
the houses of the lower upper
middle class stand by their
colored grass squares. 20 thousand dollars.
The capricious fire never threatened
those struggling properties.

When will the truck take us to eat
as the Alaska boy's friend sáid
chicken fried steak, man that's
the only good thing about this

and I tell you they got it
at the truckstop, you know how some
of it will stick in your teeth?

Sage smoke
is light, it goes off in the wind
quickly, and the smoke
of the june grass lingers
along the ground.
But this, they said,
will all be green next spring.

The wheat fields were miraculously untouched
for the ruinous flame did not leap
off the dun hill toward them.
That *storage* remains intact,
food for us does not grow,
nor is it consumed.
Those investors again chuckle,
if they think of it at all,
to see their endeavor so blessed
by a wind we thought impartial.

HOME ON THE RANGE, FEBRUARY, 1962

Flutes, and the harp on the plain
Is a distance, of pain, and waving reeds
The scale of far off trees, notes not of course
Upon a real harp but chords in the thick clouds
And the wind reaching its arms toward west yellowstone.
Moving to the east, the grass was high once, and before
White wagons moved
                    the hawk, proctor of the hills still is

Oh god did the chunky westerner think to remake this in his own
     image
Oh god did the pioneer society sanctify the responsible citizen
To do that
               face like a plot of ground
Was it iron locomotives and shovels, hand tools
And barbed wire motives for each man's
Fenced off little promised land

                         or the mind of bent

Or of carson, oh earp
These sherpas of responsible destruction
Posses led by a promising girl wielding a baton upon the street
A Sacagawea wearing a baseball cap, eating a Clark bar.
And flutes and the harp are on the plain
Bring the last leading edge of stillness
Brought no water, brought dead roots
Like an allotment of tool handles to their premises—and they cry
In pain over daily income—a hundred years of planned greed
Loving the welfare state of new barns and bean drills
Hot passion for the freedom of the dentist!
Their plots were america's first subdivisions called homesteads

Lean american—gothic quarter sections gaunt look
Managing to send their empty headed son who is a ninny
to nebraska to do it, all over again, to the ground, a prairie
Dog hole,
And always they smirk at starvation
And consider it dirty . . . a joke their daughters learn
From their new husbands.

TIME TO BURN

The great cowboy with the large round head changed his mind
and didn't like me, the thin beautiful girl crossed and
uncrossed her legs, left the table where we had been talking
and returned again not quite sure she could see me, the
cowboy objected violently when I walked from where I was the
three miles distance to where he was, the girl from the
night before simply stared as if weighing a piece of reject
stuff staring past into a distance that does no one any good.

It was 3 days to midnight

The man seemed only to be sitting with his back against the
wall, hands under the table, withholding everything, but only
from me, only my heart pleaded, as for my mouth, and my ears
they said nothing, nothing hearable, but my adam's apple moved
silently as though I was reading, while the girl as thin
as shadow left and returned, came and stayed, staring at the

Me in my heart, as if we had departed together upon a boat
certain of return to a shore where the fog shut out every
thing, and the final smile was my signal to get lost in another
part of the prairie, switched to the room where the great cowboy sat
slightly dirty and above all arrogant, smoking, alone, as if
he held uncommonly large places in his hand and didn't give a shit.

Not exactly desperate, I was leaving all the time, thwarted
for the time being, you know how it is, when you go into a
supermarket and can't find the right brand of peas?

ON THE DEBT MY MOTHER OWED TO SEARS ROEBUCK

Summer was dry, dry the garden
our beating hearts, on that farm, dry
with the rows of corn the grasshoppers
came happily to strip, in hordes, the first
thing I knew about locust was they came
dry under the foot like the breaking of
a mechanical bare heart which collapses
from an unkind an incessant word whispered
in the house of the major farmer
and the catalogue company,
from no fault of anyone
my father coming home tired
and grinning down the road, turning in
is the tank full? thinking of the horse
and my lazy arms thinking of the water
so far below the well platform.

On the debt my mother owed to sears roebuck
we brooded, she in the house, a little heavy
from too much corn meal, she
a little melancholy from the dust of the fields
in her eye, the only title she ever had to lands—
and man's ways winged their way to her through the mail
saying so much per month
so many months, this is yours, take it
take it, take it, take it
and in the corncrib, like her lives in that house
the mouse nibbled away at the cob's yellow grain
until six o'clock when her sorrows grew less
and my father came home

On the debt my mother owed to sears roebuck?
I have nothing to say, it gave me clothes to
wear to school,
and my mother brooded

in the rooms of the house, the kitchen, waiting
for the men she knew, her husband, her son
from work, from school, from the air of locusts
and dust masking the hedges of fields she knew
in her eye as a vague land where she lived,
boundaries, whose tractors chugged pulling harrows
pulling discs, pulling great yields from the earth
pulse for the armies in two hemispheres, 1943
and she was part of that *stay at home army* to keep
things going, owing that debt.

OBITUARY

Metz
dark, east, another place
a greasy plumber's cap
bent shoulders
                fixed grin
was my grandfather's
antagonist, had
the nerve to live near

and waited for
my frenchcanadian man—
                fitted pipes from tecumseh
to momence
                smoked a pipe,

but no intellectual he
graduated from
                my grandmother
used to feed
on the back steps pie
to tramps

47

                  but he
gave me a penny once
with a slick smile, big teeth

face to the wind in a motor car
down miles of track
grinning
          my grandfather did die
for that ambitious pipe fitter
next in line
a mailpouch cancer in his whispering throat

So Metz stepped
from behind the motorcar shed
in the cold January sun
                          to piss
everywhere,
his dark jaw set
in pleasant anticipatory greed
   the survey of
such small domain as
one runt dispatcher skips across

his eye set
the glint of knowing
no cancer would cancel
his scaling career with dirty pipes
cancel no trips to Segal
to Effingham
ambitious for troubling leaks
in Ficklin
trouble in Assumption, Illinois
in Teutopolis
and Altamont, those towns,
Joppa
        where my grandfather
        in the leaky waters of winter
        wasted like a job . . .

Shumway cars, St. Elmo
Elmer Chrissman, checking lackawanna cars
Metz, the happy witness of
his death
with pleasure eating mincemeat pie
at Dubois cafe
while black joe dernal in the coal pit
long black stripes on the sandwiches he
held by black fingers
lunched on flat zebras
a mid-west african
    lying in the spilled guts of a coalhopper
above the light halftoned sun
caught in the swinging steel vents oh
that was the time my grandfather died
and his helper hooked his job as death
hooked the master fitter's throat and now
the railroad too is dead

DEATH WHILE JOURNEYING

At Grinder's Stand
in his sleep
on the Natchez Trace,
in the Chickasaw country
Meriwether Lewis
had what money
and incidently his life
stole. And I never read what time of year

it was, Fall? when the papaws
drop their yellow fruit,
or Spring? and bear's grease.

Enough now
to write it down in celebration
on first reading . . .

At Grinder's Stand
on the Natchez Trace
in the Chickasaw country
an exotic place
                to die
and it fit him.

Going to see his dying mother
or was it summer,
the live oak waving
in the clear air,
but imagine,
trying to make a trip
like that alone.

. . . was given to fits
of depression Jefferson said;
is that possible? 18 whatever
6 or 7? In this case
it would be mean to be so modern

at Grinder's Stand
in the Chickasaw country
of our dreams, one century
before psychoanalysis.
After traveling transcontinent
to the Pacific then, the run-off
of ardor, Spring?
a ruminating horseback ride,
no, must have been Fall,
O Meriwether, the crisp oak leaves
under hoof, the papaw, and the smell
but most the depression, imagine
along the Natchez Trace in loneliness
to Grinder's Stand, and the ferret

Grinder, eyeing you as you passed through
the door. And an entire continent had flapped
at your coattails.

But surrounding this death
Boone had just returned to Femme Osage
with sixty beaver skins "still strong
in limb, unflinching in spirit"
standing there with a gaunt eye
watching the Astorians prepare their keel-boats,

his old ear bent
toward the Pacific tide.

But at Grinder's Stand,
which is south of Femme Osage
on the Trace, whom probably the Astorians
had nearly forgotten, a man rode in
to the final recognition
and who would have been there
                              but money-eyed

Grinder,

while the Astorians prepared their keel-boats
and Boone watched.

LEDYARD: THE EXHAUSTION OF SHEER DISTANCE

"I give up. I give up."
—JOHN LEDYARD

Around the
      Horn

with Cooke, in the swell
of the summer tides, all the trickery
one could ask for, of onslaught
one could ask for nothing more
and of course, the journals
were suppressed, though all marked
was the tenor of the passing earth,
   the jealousy
of location was the same
sheerness as the marking.

On the ghostly coast, indolent
Spaniards thought Mary could possess
by flags, the squatter's occupation
had not yet come. Still the dreamy
hurrying, Vitus Behring,
and the trip back to Petersburg
for fresh supplies, to be yoked
by scientists, those curious argumentative
people who took seven years returning
to Kamchatka,
one way. Meanwhile
the blood of the Aleuts ran
in Norton Sound, and Ledyard
regardless of the date left for Europe.

Where Jefferson said in Paris
and Jones agreed, "Go to Kamchatka
and thence across," and Ledyard went
although not a one of them had any money

52

but due to some complicated unfixing
sojourners could travel broke, tramping
as he did from Stockholm to Petersburg
around the Sea of Bothnia, and
they don't say he stopped in taverns
or what condition his shoes, the point
of destination was the Pacific coast of Russia.
This was a way to get to the other side
of America. And that must have been
no irony then. Walking is what I associate
with Ledyard, distance as sheer urge, not
satellite and its utilitarianism.

A wild, thousand mile walk
in the cold to Petersburg, thence
to Barnaul, midway with Dr. William Brown.
People were everywhere then looking
at flowers, exhibitions came long after
there was no place to go.

Where, when he got to Yakutsk
and met an old mate who had been also
with Cooke he went to Irkutsk
where Catherine's cossacks jogged up
redfaced and seized him in a confusion
of towns named Yakutsk and Irkutsk
and carried him on a horse six thousand
miles back where they set him down
just inside the Polish border, from where
probably he walked at least part of the way
back to London, which is where he said
I Give Up.

But what I wonder at times,
being only from Illinois is
did you count the stretching corridors
of spruce on that trek coming back
as we used to count telephone poles

going home from my aunt's on an endless
rainy Sunday afternoon, where shortly after
the beginning of an american siberia,
but the mystery: when did our Poland occur?
  Like your spirit
and bones to dust then
set out for the African Society
to discover the sources of the Nile
a mad Mark Antony the legions of the
weather of the earth at your back
and on the way out, fell.

Mystic sheer distance was in thine eye,
that beautiful abstract reckoning,
the feet, walking: for no other reason
the world.

LOS MINEROS

Now it is winter and the fallen snow
has made its stand on the mountains, making dunes
of white on the hills, drifting over
the flat valley floors, and the cold cover
has got us out to look for fuel.

First to Madrid which is 4 miles beyond Cerillos
close to the Golden Mountains
a place whose business once throve like the clamor in Heorot Hall;
but this was not sporting business, The Mine Explosion of 1911.
And on the wall in the mine office

                              there in Madrid

are two pictures of those blackbirds, but a time later;
the thirties, and the bite of the depression is no bleaker

on their faces than is the coming morning of the day they were
    took.
These men whom we will never know are ranged 14 in number
in one of those pictures that are very long, you've seen them.

And the wonder is five are smiling Mexicanos, the rest
could be English or German, blown to New Mexico on another
winter's snow. Hard to imagine Spanish as miners, their
sense is good-naturedly above ground (and their cruelty).
In a silly way they know their pictures are being taken,

and know it isn't necessary honor standing in line with their hands
    hiding
in their pockets. I was looking to see if they are short
as Orwell says miners must be, but they aren't save two
little Mexican boys. What caught my eye at first was the way
they were so finely dressed in old double-breasted suit coats, ready
    for work.

Then I looked into their faces and the races separated.
The English or Germans wear a look which is mystic in its
    expectancy;

able men underground,
but the Spanish face carries no emergency
and one of the little boys, standing behind a post
looks right out of the picture faintly smiling: even today. Martinez
whom I had gone with was waiting for the weight slip.
When we got over to the giant black chute the man above waved
as from the deck of a troubled ship and said no carbon
amigos, and then climbed down the ladder.

Madrid is a gaunt town now. Its houses stand unused
along the entering road, and they are all green and white,
every window has been abused with the rocks of departing children.

[1960]

IN THE MORNING

In a forgotten town
grit flies up in circles of morning dirt
and cans lie here and there on the brown earth,
a dog slips between the houses.
The sun rose large and yellow, not warm
until the taste of warmth at noon for which old men
wait, talking low tones by the brown walls
their talk thickening in that brief transport of heat.

We are pained by fetters of wind around our ankles,
yet there are no screams in this mountain town, the knife
goes deeply but cleanly each malcontent is a surgeon.
In this silent rising holocaust of down people
the garbage scrapes along in the drafts of ice
and mingles in collections on the ground, this is

their binding tie, a contribution parallel to all odds,
all eventualities—
what they have left at the end of the day
caught between walls of earth plotting

a short nervous trip to the table of another's gossip.
Somewhere near in the drifting air in
the capitol building toiled in by masses
there is a click click and a woman sitting yawns

but never in the same way stares forward
as the man in our dry town
whose wheelbarrow of wood to warn him senselessly
spills, whose wrists twist yielding to the rock
yielding to the mock buzzing of a sound economy

in the wind struggling, clad in ancient army clothes
so far from the wars.

THE LAND BELOW

The light wind falters leaves
in the cottonwood. Barely evening.
The rain earlier, coming again
from the West, in front of me.

Over the Jemez an illumined band of milk grey
where the afterglow lingers.   Nearer,
in front, a tower
two red lights come on and off.
A set for the evening.

Below the sky
the breeze is mingled with rain in New Mexico
a small sound and an earlier evening
than in Colorado, the tiers of my country
are ascending shades, but in the descending sunlight
evening comes and comes.

                        As upon

another day, before evening,
a darker one
on what kind of day,
did beautiful Hector rise
from his bed and smile,
the day his death beckoned was
it steel grey iron, and does the sun
shine early on Asia Minor?

Here, I've found it, said
Schliemann standing
in that silly silk high hat
saying I am the most
successful merchant of Petersburg, a doctor
of philosophy—why did he
for all that

bust his ass getting
a greek wife?
Do the leaves fly up in the wind
at eight o'clock along the shadows
of those hills?   this is all I care about
those commons. Of the busier
or more cardinal
human clash and clatter, the bong
of whose bells, neither you nor I care for.
Whose arm carried his armour, I asked
myself, what
must he have been like, looked
downtrodden probably, as one
today, going into battle against
all those big greezers.
And there goes Hector to work
across the plain of olives
                              I wonder
if it had come noon yet, Achilles
(mere discus thrower) killed that man
there on the coast, shame, Schliemann
did you find your pots and sherds?

But what happened to that man the arms bearer?
I still wonder what happened to that caddy.
Take your pots and sites . . .

   Let us not mention Ford workers
or generations of workers father & son
or that goddamn shit about dividing
up the land, They
who divide do so in order to
keep keep keep:
                    (They simply get
                    what they want—
                    an economy is *never*
                    more intricate
                    than that
That specific process

of standing all day by a steel
window, at a lathe, forces air
what is lying on the sidewalk
in any form
of extraction
all those Ham-tram-sick escapees . . .
not to speak of
what hybrids ach
let us leave Detroit where it is
without alarm, it is nearer Bethlehem
in a real sense, granting all strife.
You are there too, inevitably.
It all ends in not being different
than the shalestone or hunk
of lime
breaking into daylight
let us not mention ford cars
a measurement of distance is
probably not valuable.
Breaking into the shalestone
or hunk of limestone we all view
the crescent moons of shells.
Then the black outline of foliage
a finger's spread high,

                              there, moons
and leaves, we are all going
to be there
it is the backyard
of our eternity.

This is not college
or 1933. All academics are hopeless.
Glancing up
see to the north
on a spine of Earth
containing our rocks, the miles deep
fossil ranges,
containing the fragments of vertabrae

and dishy shells, really scattered
too wide,
                for an eye to offer coherence
at times,
you have to use your head as an arbiter,
a relief, for it all.

Looking up then,
in this childish vastness
(shall we make a wilderness
in which to feel alone again?)
the mica-shimmering mountains
but back, and beyond, drifting
like icebergs near the horizon, too near
the light and showered
by the light, too close
to the nether source to mention again.
The great undermine.
Nor mention age.
Exercise some restraint!

In a man's world,
there is fact.   One rises
during the day, and for a large,
but perhaps small, part of time.
The chipping off of invert reality
is alright—
                in order to peek back
everyone does this.

But let's not
so casually, image ford.
Even at all.
It is no wonder where it all came from.
Everyone wanted to build it.
Leaving aside the question
of conservation, Theodore Roosevelt
on one side, so and so on the other
let us also refrain

from talk of function, further,
empire of any sort.
This is the way to redintegration.

Indeed not be too careful . . .
how we live, hypochondria
is not becoming in a poet
any more than care, of most
sorts, freedom is not posited
upon acts, otherwise
the population of the world
would be jailed . . . lest we appear
to walk upon principles
rather than legs.   Fossils look
a great deal alike, taken in haste
from the great ranges, are more or less
undistinguishable in the sub-terra ranges
and mines earth-long and imponderably heavy.
Let, in an awareness
the different tastes of bread,
methods of baking, genre of wheat,
let us never go trudging back & forth
across hillocks in search of a "way of life"
(staff of life).

                    Rather go into Peru
as Squieres does, for a close look, taking notes
but never be afraid to say what a clammy place
Lima is, the cloud, overhead,
making a walk thru the streets laborious,
a walking stick a necessity.
Cheerfulness is still a misleading humor.
Much is blinding
besides the sun. Yet I am sure you see.
The hour is important.

Insofar as life can be lived
and can be *stated,* H D T
did well to write about it.

Became more then than living, that hapless verb.
Became a survey of more than a hubbub
of the days in which axes & bread,
ponds, window with bars out of which
to look and be disobedient, mere tools
of distraction. Altho I don't
say much for the crabby writing.
I like the clarity. Nor have much use
for the temper, but he was alive.
Knowing we can't be forever waiting for the appraisor.
In america every art has to reach toward some
clarity. That is our hope from the start.
Dicken among the indians.
A very new even surprising
element (a continent is a surprise)
makes this our reservoir of Life (not living)
Not looking back as the sluggish beast europe
at a residue of what was merely heaped up
a prepared mound, cave to go into.
Excavation.
Our possibility is to sheer off what
is only suggested.   And make anything what
soever holdable, even breezes and gasses.
Which is possibly ugly.

It is a *real* mystique, not a
mystique. A mystique of the real.
It doesn't even require a tradition
        thus
      we rid ourselves
of that cribby functionalism.
But the Comstock lode was mined in the same old way,
that's not what was meant. You will always
import old world people to work your conventional mines.
Or shoot the moon.

Somewhat funny? everyone is well-off.
But they are apt to say anytime—
don't show me the way to anything but myself.

Can that house stand?
                    Does it amaze anyone
to learn men are paid fortunes
to construct the inevitable.

                    Yes,
any kind of house
will stand.   Principles are very misleading.
Once you have found one or two
you can build a library let alone a house.
Take 1931-1941 as a decade.   It is funny now,
so effete. When you see one of those old
people riding a horse with a red saddle
through the streets shouting "Times Change"—
What a lie.   They do not change.   Or,
have not.

They say "Well, Stevenson
speaks well, is at home
with ideas (yi) . . . why can't it be
why can't we have a good man
what the hell is wrong, son of a bitch
I'd like to tear somebody's throat out
Geezchrist, but he does speak eloquently."

One cries for the night, and
the moon,
when such figures are a little obscured
at least it is a moment when the seeing
of this slime
is a little obscured.
It comes on in the late afternoon of the spirit,
one comforts one's children and looks aimlessly out the window
for perhaps the last time.
A friend comes and perhaps one talks on.

This is a record of these days.
Sometimes the days end happily
in scotch, this is rare, and when
the invitation comes and you are actually there

on your way to the bathrooms of the rich
(the stool is the exact height Lewis Mumford proposed)
for relief you see there is so much left,
and that an untampered bottle waits
in its oak or hickory ease
further back, casually, by the window.
It will *never* end, busy people are busy importing it,
and no matter how far, the desert, the mountains,
the river, the sea.

And the Younger generation
that post teen flab which
has eyed this hunk of dirt
called Earth (and didn't
make it till yesterday)—
they are even funnier. Castro
The revolutionist.   It is
suddenly as if Machiavelli hadn't existed
hadn't said a word, didn't tell us everything
on the subject worth knowing
for ever.   From now actually unto eternity.
That any slob can suddenly ride up in a limousine
and tell us anything, is
one of the world's true wonders.

At this point I am thirty.
Yesterday a man my elder accused me of doing nothing.
You could work, he said.
        Transfer of knowledge: much like the stranded semi
        one sees the flares, but there is no chance to see
        the cargo, that dissemination I
        or you, are on the last
        diminishing end of,
        where we all receive covered goods.

It is like a protection racket.
Temptation is so manifest
even a justicer can see it.
Ride a beautiful horse

with a red saddle through the streets.
But starkness too is manifest.   There are
no silver hounds at our feet.   Once in Dodona
perhaps . . . but not anymore.

To the North
we traveled along
with other cars.
The day was hot,
the desert rolled before us

and in our way we marveled
at faint buttes—
the horizon was a tapestry that day.
Contours, even driving I saw
much of its passing aspect
from the cockpit of the car.
Cloud's shadows,
the changing colors, dark green juniper
and looser colors, the dun of terra
the sharper brown of rock mounds and
to Taos we finally came.

Didn't know we were to see a wonderful man
earlier this afternoon
standing in God's waning light
at the end of San Francisco street,
the children in Disney's hands,
Sleeping Beauty,
I saw Christ in a kit.
Like a travel kit.
You were to zip open the case
there was the cross laid
in the middle with a gold Jesus,
in another depression of the foam rubber
was a bottle of water, on the other side
there were candles.

Looming over gigantically
in the same window

a smirking Christ
made effeminate as always
in a southern latitude
where women are nice
there were his incredibly long and slender toes.
The hands pointing to
a decorated rouge heart.
Holes pierced his hands.
Incredibly long fingers like the toes
curled hair
but the smirk
perhaps more just than I then thought.
The picture:
three people walk
upon an automobile
lined street,
an overdraft of senses
coming from
our lovely Earth.
The tallest,
the man in the center walking
a beret
on his head
            a beret—
the boy,
in a sailor cap
old word habiliment
hand on a sign
the foot of the boy on the image
of our Earth
he can feel it, the concrete covers it.

The woman, on their left.

At the curb,
the licensed car—California the island
sits there, California
far away.

The woman on the right.

Descending shadow lines
long in back
along the buildings sit
my sighting
in grey sunlight
within the polished paper
without ever hoping to touch it
without my fingers
on the fragile fire escapes
the black latticework of New York City.
Without being there.

The woman carries
hanging from her shoulder
something from Tepic
my friend these years
yet whom I have seen
but one time,
during an almost quiet week
where the street
and descending shadows
the bulks
going back out,
through a door,
going back out
down stairs
                    (and John W's and H. and I
                    saw Jackie Cooper standing
                    smiling hangover, on the corner
                    in little black loafers,
                    with tasseled strings . . .

They are all walking
in front of me
like a far away call
not cavalry upon plains
but the silence

from a sidewalk, looking down
the feet are so visible
as the automobiles herded in lines—
gross impinging
at rest happily.
No fear have I
but I have the picture
propped against a quart jar.

The woman,
her look, remain so young.
A stratum of the
presence of man.

Three others:
one real-estate merchant
one owner
one bystander (buyer?)
in the lot below,
disposal so complete
is quite unbelievable
. . . the manner in which they dispense
with our world, i.e.,
how did we come to invade it, how
did we get
here, in their clutches, where are
we to go?   save
to a house of their possession
as objects, "renters"
when will it come.
One month, or an hour
to the disposal.

The adobe is 100 yrs. old
I am thirty
my wife thirty-two
3 children—one 5 (boy
        " 8 (girl
        " 10 boy)

The striking thing
the truth of falsehood, I hadn't believed,
yet the selling is going on in that

             vacant
        lot
where Lot's wife, looking on
would again be turned to salt.
This world I did tread upon *is*
in their waxed palm. Whole sections
not only gold coins, stick to it
and are raised up into the air.

Befouling all *other* worlds.
"That coyote put a deal of real estate between
himself . . ." and whoever . . . that's Mark Twain.

But worlds do come together, like science
and as science, the cartoon anarchist
black cloak
and great rimmed hat
renting a hole where they stand
(remember to light the wick)
deeds and surveys and plan.

They are so pale
looking from the car window
going by,
the glance is sideways
that roar, the jet
not fast, no jazz,
and not high, so close
to Earth, on it in fact
the dancing arm flung up
to rest on the back of the seat,
but the paleness, they are
another race. One wants
wants to go with them in the seat
riding shotgun

surging ahead although there would be nothing
duller.
        Because it is all in the flash
and black sideburn
their small flickering corner of real life.
You, are not there.   A myopia
where everything is passing—
how about those fur dice
and roman hubcaps?
Nothing is for the voyeur, one wouldn't think
of laughing, as you would at a common parade.

Fourth of July
at the plaza, there
was supposed to be a parade
but there were only advertising
milk cow floats, sports cars carrying broads
& flags driven by fags,

then these creatures I have brought to you
circling circling, the plaza.

How everyone was not seeing
the most subtle thing, I mean
there were fords at last
roaring, that paleness, oh
it isn't that the rest are vapid
and loathsome clothed people
carrying baskets got there by false
expectations (as it turned out there was
no parade) huge hats, and they were pale
too, pastel portraitures on the lawn
under the trees, and the chief of police
in a cart drawn by an ass, who one woman
told me coyly, annually stole 3 thousand
from the rodeo till, there was this protected
fondled almost bonded bit of nice pleasant
corruption for a town that likes to play
eccentric.

And the true chief
the real one who picks up
all the women in a pick-up
at night when they have put the trinkets
used to lure the white man from Iowa
back in their bags.

But the circling,
the roaring Chucs
of a modern fourth of July
where they all start out
and end up nowhere
like the dark eye on the bench,
burning eyes, a very
long slit, sitting
beautifully in a respect,
how did he get so far north, who?
transplanted him (with what
                    so called historical
                    gesture of trade & slavery
brought
him into a clatter he can't even hear.

As we came down
                    into the green pines
the sharp brushes raking our faces
greeted by cooler air,
the children ran on
                    looking
for a table.
Walking on the path
I saw alders again. Very good.
We were on the revolutionary earth—
"Take this table" the woman called
from under the tree and we walked over
to sit down, as they moved their things
to another table, where an old man sat.

He wore a green shirt, otherwise
he retained a solitude, his lean ankles crossed.
And the hair done up in back
with a simple white tight wound cloth
and girding his hair and forehead
a patterned handkerchief, a forelock hanging
over, the longer hair bobbed around his head.
There was a chipmunk stealing wieners,
the fastness a cartoon movement, was such
a difference looking from it to the man.

Borrowing a light from their fire
I stood and smoked, the women joked
pleasantly, laughing much, it would
cost a dime for the light, it was going
to rain, they had just performed a dance,
they might even scalp us (noticing the
whiteness of the children's hair). But the Old Man
hardly smiled, at least one couldn't tell,
the grimness of his lips, I felt my scalp tingle,
did it engage his memory?

But having had a light from an ember
and standing there, I marveled at the beauty
of men who have long hair.   Yes, it is quite
different.   Their world.   I am sure they tread
upon an Earth I don't. And I would like to.
Not facilely, or for long, but to be with them
for a spell, the chatter
of the woman really distraction, everything
they had, gone up in smoke.   It must have been their idea
to camp, imagine, indians camping.

Playing indian.   They take too lightly
their breed, forcing me to take too lightly
what I am.   But ah,
the man is so old, has emphatically not
made the change as they
in their tapered pants.

Was not thinking of any catechism, at all.
Very little concerned if everything changes to cobalt.
And wouldn't have yearned for the lime-secreting pre-cambrian
algae, not using lime stone, as a product.

But Beauty is remarkable in that you
can never return to it.   It never
exists again, once having been there.
And this instant I relate; this long
haired, slow to look creature, sitting once again
ankles crossed at a bench—only their heads remain,
from the gullet down, that dull gondola,
the automatic body, is just like ours
would you believe it, scoffing wieners
and 7 up.

HAWTHORNE, END OF MARCH, 1962

That day was dark.
Fog fell down our mountain.
The snows were wet patches
and around the legs
laid as lichen around the barn's
stark red shadows.

The day he died—
the slow quiet break.
What an odd person to die beside: Franklin Pierce.
Never go to the mountains.
Near the end, the air
is spoken for.
I thought how just; americans
still love morally with many preliminary questions.

   He was fierce
for the slight connection
back to what
         there was.

THE SONG IS ENDED

for Nellie L.

Lingers on
but the
melody when everyone goes
the moon

we sang, to say
too soon
and found that everyone
too soon
had gone
with the moon

Do you
        love
me baby
like you used to now
I'd like to know
Oh I'd like to know

IN MY YOUTH I WAS A TIRELESS DANCER

But now I pass
graveyards in a car.
The dead lie,
unsuperstitiously,
with their feet toward me—
please forgive me for
saying the tombstones would not
fancy their faces turned from the highway.

Oh perish the thought
I was thinking in that moment
Newman Illinois
the Saturday night dance—
what a life!   Would I like it again?
No.   Once I returned late summer
from California thin from journeying
and the girls were not the same.
You'll say that's natural
they had been dancing all the time.

THE PRONOUNCEMENT

What had flat mud roofs and bare cottonwoods meant to me
making a fixture in my eye of this mindless spell?
Where I was born stalwart black winter's snows stay on roofs
week after week, the roofs are slanted making planes of blue
and red, the various greens are the memory of elms and summer
looked to save everything and grow the people's garden patches.

Here, though, the air stays bright all winter and brighter even
are the mountains and before them the supporting hills glow.
Across town the vivid Shriners' tabernacle, startlingly
of brick, and red tiled roofs, an anonymous 18th century engraving.
The quietness is impossible to resist:
Reading Patchen and pails of soldiers' livers, the butchering
laughter of Winston Churchill seems a familiar and tiring cry
of another time making the road to Wigan Pier with Orwell
something to transport the spirit to common sense.   Traveling
in the Congo with Gide, 1927, all a life of impression
where the observation becomes the life of the object (a strange
sense of Nothing) the removals
are what I am trying to pronounce, that they
are my case.

And sitting here on my porch, one can see so far across
the supporting hills to Los Alamos, a quietness almost too deep
to hear, but one which gives its sound, visually, in the rising
smoke of its various technical plantations of death.
A slow and unrevealing line about myself curls up from an Alamos
chimney and my understanding nature darts like a borzoi away.
Such a thing as humanity seems very relative, the final
abjuring of any vision.   Again to know:
What factor comes like an arrow to locate us?

Then, from a newly opened box of old books, fished out Pound and/or
Jefferson and/or mussolini and got weary for hours under that
ceaseless prating (the unhappy function of "style") beneath a shiny
veneer of precise common logic and raw virtue and good nature

76

yes, that book is good-natured too.   But it now comes down
like all news, like a curtain on a comedy.

After all these pronouncements: What I already knew: not a damn
    thing
ever changes: the cogs that turn this machine are set
a thousand miles on plumb, beneath the range of the Himalayas.

A TOO HOPEFULLY BOLD MEASURE

The snow lies against the slope
as skin clings to a baby giraffe
spotted here and there with clumps
the neck of our yearning is the hope of other animals
the breathing of the earth is dispelled
as the clumps of juniper tremble
in the breeze.

The worker on share deludes his fingers
in the sole nets of alaska waters
or the cane fields and the island breezes
pass around the fingers and cane
crying that all are screwed
with all economies

so fleshlessly do they inaugurate themselves
over the land, do they come from the aspirations
of men clothed in soft wool
of steel dividends, ties of china silk
which china?   which necks?
who hawks the goods to wetbacks
in the freezing breezes of the borders.

Has the mass changed since the 19th century
can we spin Jack London around
in a game of blind man's bluff

no more for gold we are the fools of—
their bottomless pockets from
the dry washes drummed by star corporations
like not masses but the tabulations
we are, haunt the stone architect barracks
housing the manifest destiny of Rand
run across the earth one last time, be that horde
again in the deadly angelic face of pure gratuitous
extempore planned putrifacted and revived breathing:

And by such bold measures massage a stopped heart
out of the rancor to please,
like a woman
against what is the most loved curving.

THE ENCOUNTER

The reach is sudden.
I heard of Harvey today.
The news is
11 years old.
A man spoke
at the end of a conversation
"we were in Vantage Washington
yesterday, my informant
said he knew you too."

There was a laurel bush
15 feet high by the door

where I lived back then.
The softness of greeting
and the light of his laugh.
They said a dying bird
was in his cornea.
It may be there were doric
columns inside his ears.

His world was unluckily confused.
He always shook his head without speaking.

HEMLOCKS

Red house.   Green tree in mist.
How many fir long hours.
How that split wood
warmed us. How continuous.
Red house.   Green tree I miss.
The first snow came in October.
Always.   For three years.
And sat on our shoulders.
That clean grey sky.
That fine curtain of rain
like nice lace held our faces
up, in it, a kerchief for the nose
of softest rain.   Red house.

Those green mists rolling
down the hill.   Held our heads
when we went walking on the hills
to the side, with pleasure.
But sad.   That's sad.   That tall grass.
Toggenburg goat stood in, looking, chewing.
Time was its cud.

Red barn mist of our green trees of Him
who locks our nature in His deep nature
how continuous do we die to come down
as rain; that land's refrain
no we never go there anymore.

TIME BLONDE

She was a figurine moving
among the hills of seattle
experimentally clothed
she drove an experimental car
to the stores.

What was life then?

It was wandering between
the planted trees of a climate
of light red rain, it was
just the going to and fro
in a light cold climate
hoping to meet, but nothing said,
to bed, if she had the time.

By which I mean didn't we
wait much of the time staring out
at the various parts of the city
and during those nights
of waiting
the little red lights
in the water of the bays
did they not say no use?

UNLIKE MUSIC

The book
   was scattered through
     with notes

Unlike music
   which is a line
     of unfixed sound

of bridges
   through silence
     a structure of footings

the notebook
   was scattered through with blue
ink,
     a dead web

and held in place
small pieces of his life
that he had bought

the chickens
   bred the rabbits
     sold the calf
       sold the goat

there were no dates
or marks of when,

and no melody
to recur to him
   no recourse

backward
   a life
going away like snows

on the mountains in the cold
of great altitudes, he was

the yellow man in the book.

OH DON'T ASK WHY
(*for H.*)

The preparations repeated
the stove lids lifted
lifted, coal gas
billows
up
    When in a large heated public
building, how warm
no wonder how warm

The eye of the beholder is not
only
not necessary

irrelevant testimony to how
curiously we can live our days
Were we asked?

Certainly not
    That sun, did it come
to warm only us? I think
so
    But repeatedly
I don't know

How you loved me
through all travesty
how you kept those lovely eyes
clear,

their burn
fixed away from some
monument of curiosity,—How
ever can you live like that?

Yes, at moments I did waste
our lives, giving way
foolishly to public thoughts,
large populations.

Are we needed?   On this mountain
or in this little spud town in the valley
or along this highway, you held
your eyes on getting us there, repeatedly
where?   We

never knew
but now do and what is it
in this small room so bitter
an image of time at times
keeps us from falling
into that religious cry
of I'm not here!
but which we now transpose
with an old hope
we scoured the ground of the earth
to start fires
in these rickety geographies
we knew better than to call home

from smiling
to hiding true thoughts
true feeling as an inner lining
against the cold and secret medicines

heat and water, light
for the lonely comes only as a fringe benefit

Carry geology in the eye
though nobody calls you long distance
to learn the nature of that terrain
Oh don't ask why the welcome signs remain.

A FATE OF UNANNOUNCED YEARS

I will have to pick my cluster of grapes
in this country,
after everyone else has gone
to Korcula or Spain.   It will be strange
here, walking through the parks, the folding
chairs gone, the meandering lovers
and old women in their Sunday hats gone;
an empty air, and a peaceful kind of rest.
Finding myself in america
slowly walking around the deserted bandstand, waiting
for the decade, and the facetious new arrivals.

HANDS UP

Out west
desperadoes are only desperate
and brown pastures
are there our battles

with hands off, nature
let me be
one who, as I can
turn green, russet
tan and gold
let mine eyes turn
to mountains with patches
yellow subsidy
with the famous indian
sitting sulky
in the cold shack
surculose, that word,
please pass the dignity
under the gale from that
inland sea
where covered wagons
cloud above could
have come, with sails
across wyoming, no, no
there seems no heat
to ward it off, but hands
across my gale
off my or your neck
wandering as a hopefully
looking goose
her hiss
this place where friends
cremate each other
to make room
      and phosphate,
is one lucky factoryowner's
element.

FROM GLOUCESTER OUT

It has all
come back today.
That memory for me is nothing
there ever was,
                    That man

so long,
when stretched out
and so bold
                    on his ground
and so much
lonely anywhere.

But never to forget
                    that moment

when we came out of the tavern
and wandered through the carnival.
They were playing
the washington post march
but I mistook it for manhattan beach
for all around were the colored lights
of delirium
                    to the left the boats
of Italians
and ahead of us, past the shoulders
of St. Peter the magician of those fishermen

the bay
stood, and immediately in it the silent
inclined pole where tomorrow the young men
of this colony
so dangerous on the street
will fall harmlessly
into the water.

They are not the solid
but are the solidly built
citizens, and they are about us
as we walk across
                    the square
with their black provocative
women
slender, like whips of
sex in the sousa filled night.

Where edged
by that man in the music
of a transplanted time and
enough of drunkenness
to make you senseless of all
but virtue
                (there is never
no, there is never a small complaint)
(that all things shit poverty,
and Life, one wars on with
many embraces) oh it was a time that was perfect
but for my own hesitating
to know all I had not known.
Pure existence, even in the crowds
I love
will never be possible for me

even with the men I love
                        This is
the guilt
that kills me
                My adulterated presence

but please believe with all men
I love to be

•

That memory
of how he lay out

on the floor in his great length
and when morning came,
late,
we lingered
in the vastest of all cities
in this hemisphere
                    and all other movement
stopped, nowhere
else was there a stirring known to us

yet that morning I stood
by the window up 3 levels
and watched a game
of stick ball, thinking of going away,
and wondering what would befall that man
when he returned to his territory.
The street as you could guess
was thick with their running
and cars,
themselves, paid that activity
such respect I thought a ritual
in the truest sense,
where all time and all motion
part around the space of men
in that act
as does a river flow past
the large rock.

            •

And he slept.
in the next room, waiting
in an outward slumber
                    for the time

we climbed into the car, accepting all things
from love, the currency of which is
parting, and glancing.

Then went
out of that city to jersey

88

where instantly we could not find our way
and the maze of the outlands west
starts that quick
where you may touch
your finger to liberty
and look so short a space
to the columnar bust
of New York
and know those people exist
as a speck in your own lonely heart
who will shortly depart,
taking a conveyance for the
radial stretches
past girls on corners
past drugstores, tired hesitant
creatures who I also love
in all their alienation were it not so
past all equipment of country side
to temporary homes
where the wash of sea and other
populations come
once more to whisper only one thing
for all people: a late and far-away
night yearning for
and when he gets there
I want him to stay away
from the taverns of familiarity
I want him to walk by the seashore alone
in all height
which is nothing more than
a mountain. Or the hailing of a mast
with big bright eyes.

So rushing,
            all the senses
come to him
as a swarm of golden bees
and their sting is the power
he uses as parts of

the oldest brain. He hears
the delicate thrush
of the water attacking
He hears the cries, falling gulls
and watches silently the gesture of grey
bygone people. He hears their cries
and messages, he never

ignores any sound.
As they come to him he places them
puts clothes upon them
and gives them their place
in their new explanation, there is never
a lost time, nor any inhabitant
of that time to go split by prisms or unplaced
and unattended,
                    that you may believe

is the breath he gives
the great already occurred and nightly beginning world.
So with the populace of his mind
you think his nights? are not
lonely. My God. Of his
loves, you know nothing and of his
false beginning
you can know nothing,
                    but this thing to be marked
again

      only

he who worships the gods with his strictness
can be of their company
the cat and the animals, the bird he took
from the radiator
of my car saying it had died
a natural death, rarely seen in a bird.

To play, as areal particulars can out of the span
of Man, and of all, this man

does not
      he, does, he
  walks
      by the sea
in my memory

and sees all things and to him
are presented at night
the whispers of the most flung shores
from Gloucester out

                  [1964]

SONG: THE ASTRONAUTS

for clair oursler

On the bed of the vast promiscuity
of the poet's senses is turned
the multiple world, no love is possible
that has not received the
freight of that fact
no wake permissible that has not met
the fluxes of those oceans.
the moon orbits
only for that permission.
Men with fine bones in their heads
will manipulate a recovery
and put spades into her
only to find Euripides went before them
          the hymen long ago fixed
it is an old old wedding
but as you dig you will not hear
the marriage flutes
you will be killed in your sleep.

Broken.
you will be considered pirates
and killed when Hymenaeus
(who lost his voice and life
                    singing at a wedding
catches you asleep
in the rushes of
the windless moon

            the immensely soft glow of it
            will always be behind you
            as you stand on its face
                    staring
                at the strangely
            inhabited world
                    from whence you came
            from where all men with their eyes
            have been satisfied

                before thee

THE PROBLEM OF THE POEM
FOR MY DAUGHTER, LEFT UNSOLVED

The darkness rings.
                the surface form
        of the face, a halo
of the face,
as it passes away in the air as she moves
    between the buildings, a cut
    surrounding her throat, the pearls
    of the price she'll never have to insist
she paid

a thin line red with its own distinction
some goiter
of what she has been made to understand is civilization
not the brand of the adventurous cutlass

The misery is superficial now.
I have dwelt on that quality in other poems
without attention to the obvious
drain
          of social definition
the oblivious process
of a brutal economic calculus, where to
                                        place the dark hair
save above moist eyes
the black slacks,
the desperately optimistic rouge of the fallen cheeks
                              (cheeks are up
when they live
              both forward *and*
posterior, the colorado of new day not a new state . . .
where the leads are I despair to find lead mines

                    In the chronically vast complex
explanation, a field true,
but a field
no field hand knows
beyond the produce of it
      on some citizen's land, the horizons
sheer the top
   of the head of the man
      who is bent
      bent is an attitude
   I've settled on now
        to define a man
   whose attention is forced down
   a class, distracted, not a stratum
   detained from what the reaper called attention
        might harvest, O false shift of season
   in a vacation

but how slow, and seasonal
and the poem is an instrument of intellection
thus a condition
of the simultaneous
so the woman and myself, pass,
and her message bears a huge meanness
                    "the measureless crudity of the States"

A world where no thing thrives short of the total pestilence
of its spirit, and because there is no intelligence short
of the total there is no intelligence, none. There is not even one
intelligence in the land, children see the capitol of things
shifted to disneyland, no misery
which does not know all misery,
as an eye of knowledge, contrary to happiness
that quite exclusive short range and burst, as it happens
a birthday party, my daughter's. I had gone to the supermarket
for ice cream.   and saw the shocked woman

     We call the intersection of time
and event the
devastation of a fortune cake
all answers pulled out
of the standard of living which is that cake
no standard is cake
a provided nation
is no standard, rather a thorn
in the side of a more careful world
     her pain affirmed (all men and women
who suffer deeply, in any way, are not
cannot be U.S. Citizens, no matter where
they live. They may live in Indiana
     she carried no standard,
     as I saw her: impossible to be a citizen
     there is no such thing anywhere, in any country.
   I could have shot her down, had she been a marine.
She was a housewife.

And leaving the scene, and the legal questions
not one male canaanite would have come forward
She was no phoenician raped broad,
there are never any ships parked by the bannock county court house
this woman was sometime willingly captured by another,
a sort of community, her husband, if she is unfortunate enough
        to possess one
is probably a masonic reservist.

·   No woman is Helena
unless the culture has provided for the passage of pain
and no people can construct the delicacies of culture
unless they imagine Helena, merely fucking in the middle
of the atlantic on the SS *United States* is not it, is procurement
while the full-sized poodle whines in the kennel above
back of the forward stack, the echo of the sound he makes in
        Berkeley
where the hippest member of the minority group as it was reported
arrived in a sports car and there it was, white, with a beret
wearing shades, sitting beside the driver, looking with disdain
on a small cur who trotted along the curb and stopped
for one brief moment of curiosity and then resumed
his policing of the bases of parking meters

        These United States.
have sent forth women, hopeless divorcees,
the wrinkled millionairesses of resources dwindled
to a day dream, the exhausted mesaba of their dangling breasts
soft wax structures to support our collectively ceaseless greed
for legitimate youth, but divided states do not create women,
Amelia Earhart
was not carried off, she flew, like something familiarly
transvestite in us, a weirdly technical Icarus
she was sent for by some morse-code spiritism, this land
was never more than the bitter hardness of nouns for us
her destiny was not qualified by myth
                                She came in all her beauty
to a small green island
in a bag of metal, oh misfortune that to be exemplary is so difficult
she could have been a goddess because she flew, other women

95

marked by sex, fold out of the minds of american men
who may no longer wear the bottoms of their trousers rolled
but who are certainly all circumcised without ritual
and wear the ends of their penises rolled
and always assure their dentists they are masturbators:
                                             the paraphernalia
of an existence, thus a human phenomenon, culture-less
(pop culture,
             technologically provisioned
(those are collections of people grasping nothing
                                       the women are
                       set loose to walk spiritless
their marks are deep cuts on the neck, moist eyes, sagging nylons
eyes painted to dry everything, loose figures of despair
or hard flesh prolonged by injections and tucks into an isolated youngness
a manufactured Galateability
                             The end
                             of applied genetics will be
                          / the elimination of freely disposed
                             intellection, via the rule
                             that a science is oriented toward
                                   Use, some predictable
                       breed, is the end
(Automation ends with a moral proposition, THE LESSON of
one maximum factor of it
will suggest all the correspondences:
                             mail food ads
                             the attractive stuffing
                             from *McCalls* and *House Beautiful*
                             to Havana
                                       during any season
       of famine, therefore those people will hunger more
       (which people?
       the natural seedbed of that morality
       is plague, and all such endeavor
       instructs one to move our daughters
       to some green island
          in the sea, we are so far from Galilee
The sum of her

shall perish, has begun
to perish in the darkside
in the prescribed field of misery
and she will hardly avoid the destruction
of her nature,
a material of birth
as a car of new life
   not new, novel, the life
   is older than that we know as prima materia
     And soon when there is no need
for waitresses, or telephones, doctors' wives
and automobilists, they wither
on their still green vine, no more tears
to water life, no more varicose veins
the Kaddish will be said
not as a formal memory
but for the working of a curse, venus
will be likewise a disease transmitted for a secure experience
a memory of Eve for some isolated engineer
who said if I don't do it, someone else will
   A man,
   in that framed condition
   of some totally onanized culture, who will
   transmit with the bills of requisition
   the bill that held Leda off the ground
   in that throbbing moment when she saw histories of the future
   in the bright feathers, knew the spines of
   that ancient creature in her thighs

   the engineer's note:
Send me a little syphilis this month,
                 I have been reading
                   some old books

and in that sense
there is no loss to *a* man
of his earlier knowledge,
a yawn simply defines the brink of availability:
                Hello there Ed, congratulations!

I've forgotten the *details*
but it sounded *fabulous*!

It is the night of the opening
of the new art-grocerystore and all the shoppers
were discussing theology, a science which has no subject-matter,
something about the indistinguishability of environment where all
the mistakes of logic create a different object, something
without tears, something

as I get it less like
the terrestrial entry a cave or
less similar volcano than woman
something omitting holes
a specifically anti metaphorical being
like a man protruding, an extension
no intention, space is still not conceived
(as surrounding: infinity is the inability
to conceive, the collapse
of surrounding,
female principle was structure
before and somewhat after the opening
of the art-grocerystore

So tears, or the rose enfolds
the moisture of its passion
the girl my daughter, 14 today
and such eyes, all interior, a proud thing
born in 1951, not yet bestowed with any curse, she is
Chansonette, a woman, hopefully, for nomads
a principle older than man, a running out
the tear dropped into an earth rapidly drying tonight,
the disappearance instant
into the most unimaginable laundromat, the danger
a wholly adjectival father might worry over
in the nest of the most corrupted notion thus far: America!
of how men might, if they were noble
behave in their last moments we barely speak
except for the relatively sour hope that some nineteenth century
and romantically singular form of bloodletting

be reinstated because the man in the street hears a choir
of pioneers' voices and thinks of brigadiers when a rightist is hurt
where he sits on the porch of his finca faraway
                                        or of how we might
plead our case in the face of Sartre's observation
that this is a nation where those who care
are the damned of the earth, *running* I will add
before the furious nations who snap at our heels
with a momentum of the centuries, and I stand
behind the pane at my window one of those hopeless men, some
        silly toscanini
leading the symphony
in the street, directing the movements, I do so know
all the scores by heart, by a memory
saturated with defeat, where crisis and alienation
are no more new than any other condition but were always
bred in this strewn and used land, no cultural tricks of assimilation
to form a cover,
                bunchgrass is an isolated cover,
has a slight brief flower,
and I can tell my daughter no secret.

A LETTER, IN THE MEANTIME,
NOT TO BE MAILED, TONIGHT

The arm swings
and the tracery
of its arc is
of the same breed
of immense
                emotion
    as the horizon on a blue morning
Art wounded in this theocracy

we can no longer be held together
by the mere terms
the mere conditions
of our captivity
the arrow of the art passes through our centers
and it used to leave us amazed at the rapport
of our mutual singular disaffection.

                              In this Theocracy
headed by the texan in buckled shoes
and the popart grin and surrounded by women
with all those funny embarrassing names we saw men murdered
and maimed on TV, and waited to hear the smug explanations
and shouted our derisive punctuations while the picture
and the voice played on played on and later went downstairs
into the parlor of that lame Wittgensteinian and tried
on his defective record player to hear Snooks Eaglin.
Thus we practiced assiduously and mutually an extension
of that Art
designed by more apt men than we were then
to keep us apart but more than that, to keep
our senses apart, to make dormant at least
and at best to make wrecked
to have made inoperative the mechanism
                                     whereby we track
with the capturing powers of our own love
the expanding universe, as it goes
in our brief time beyond us, as we reach
the black dot in our eyes, for that largeness
the interruption of nothing else could matter.

                              Let's take it
from another letter: To be agitated *is* to be involved
in this Theocracy where the *Structure* has rotted—
no Bible state and not that scheme which anyone
might understand to get in or out of, and
it is nerves it all goes to, the language does not help
because there is too much slack from that to its source
in reference to the first real utterance, nerves is
precisely what is left of God
                              as State

100

I agree with everybody in this cold longitude. Everyone
is right, ripe that word means, this evening is as
false as that evening we spent in wyoming with the man
we went to see, and who else, of *all* people to all
places could have beckoned us thither save him, of Buffalo
and that air so dry in the eye of its wetness and infertile
to an extreme we almost drunk ourselves to death with
who because he could not otherwise explain left
                                          the next day
and took all the gods with him
                        however
this letter is to a black man from whom I have become separated
in a newest of all land with the oldest hyphen of the western world
hot wet rooms where everyone ages rapidly, and we said pragmatic
goodbyes,
            a tension of action which all things become in forlorn places
where some outcast people find a place at last and others wander
with an open and unplaceable heart in this most enforced of all
        wildernesses.

INAUGURATION POEM #2

1

Behind all the trees in America there are men standing
and they are spooks, they are the men and the women,
and the children who look around, past the dirty protective bark
hiding the filth of our days here, the cover
of what we have done with a rope and a knife and a chair and
        chamber
on crossroads at night, in the apertures of alleys, in the backs
of restaurants, on mesas with broadbrimmed former athlete
and presently cowboylooking, or, the boy in the vocational program
today will be the sheriff and the petty hood, his equipotential
tomorrow, the cover of what we have done. Everyone knows our
        benevolence
but not everyone knows our benevolence was always well grounded
in a base of return, not gain, for God's sake, that
was never enough, but return, wall street is no miss named

101

it does separate, it does wall our gigantic society off
it marks us apart from where we are, I don't mean it as
a joke, Ah uz not jokin, mah boy married a heebrew, do they
let them heebrews go onto the sahara desert or are they only arabs
there? But they are Spooks.
Spooks is not a misnomer. Indians are spooks too.
Lovers are spooks and communists are spooks in america
like Trotsky is a spook in mexico, only Rightists are real
thus their blood must be let so they can be spooks too
so they can be americans too, because if you aren't a spook
you are *not* an american. Poets are spooks.
Negro poets are the spookiest biggers.
Buggers are Biggers.
The Bigger the better? The University of Alabama football team
they take the sperm of a universe they want to deny
into their open uptilted mouths every time they play, it drips
whether he knows it or not
across the white pearly acres of the quarterback's teeth,
that is the field he truly plays upon, there is where
those signals are called.
                    And so,

upon this cold January day,
in a heated box of glass, here I am without a coat on, the trees
have been sprayed with a chemical which is the private property
of a local Washington tree-sprayer, to keep the feet
of starlings off the branches
above, the spectators, as if the starlings wanted to attend that badly
or gave a shit, carry 20 dollar bills in their beaks, and sit
on the seats below. Sheriff Rainey could come if he wanted
on a bus eating popcorn, but the starlings, who were *invited*
several decades ago to this hemisphere will get the hot-foot
no hot-dogs, suggestively enough, and in-spite-of-all baseball
into the mouths of the southerners who ride the fronts of busses.

Next time, don't marry a jew, and don't hire the man with the beard
and don't bring niggers to hoe your cheapshit cotton, but for that
matter don't get some bespeckled idiot from new england to set blades
so seeds can be &c, you will always find that those people black
or white, will breed like hell once they get jobs, and get those spicks

102

out of Imperial and places like St. Paul minnesota, and Laguna
    california
How could 190 million Americans have been so thick fingered!

Those are the troubles simply put—
                                OH Mr. Johnson
when you take your war on poverty to Inez Kentucky,
to the tarpaper shacks, don't look into every face, don't shake every
    hand,
don't look ahead to a bright highway of hope
for the impoverished and unemployed of the nation, please
pass some laws so the 8 to 12 thousand-a-year (those excluded are
    unintentioned
pinhead can pinch the ass off his colleague and build cabins
near hemingway's grave in ketchum in peace
                                and when you mount the
    rude
steps of the cabin of Tom Fletcher take your secret service men with
    you
so they may spit and fume on his unwashed presence, let them tell him
because they know, he's a little, unimportant man, let them watch him,
his every poor, defeated, loser's, hopeless move, loser, buried
in verbiage. Surrounded by wadding, his sons
                                need
a college education, they know better, they know he needs a bath.
                                                        Don't
say anything to him, jobless,
who earned 400 dollars last year scratching for coal on the surface
of neighboring hills, you in a neatly pressed business suit and he Tom
    Fletcher
in khaki trousers and tattered sport shirt a gust of wind knocking over
the privy door, in ten minutes of chatting, mrs. johnson engrossed
in talk, slop on the floor, neat of course, the poor are always said to be
neater than anyone else, poor but honest, or that age-old bullshit about
mended clothes, if they are neat and clean being as good as, if not better
than the clothes of the rich whom you OH AMERICANS
stand before. Take care of yourselves, said Johnson, as he left the
    hillside cabin
and don't you forget now, I want you to put those boys through
    school.

103

2

Americans, you were that stupid from the beginning the rest of the
    world
stood with their lower jaws dead with amazement at you, and you
    never
never did get that the point from the beginning, Columbus, Cabot,
Nuñez, LaSalle, Estavanico, the Kid, was precisely non-
rational, you really thought you had to annihilate the Narraganset
which means people of the small point, oh god, the moon, is the body
of the small point, your whole concern is of small point, the war
saw concerto seems to your crossed eyes a song of great emotion
But you missed it, they made no images; their divinities
were ghosts; they were extreme spiritualists. Plenty of gods
The Sunn
            Moone,
                    Fire,
Water,
        Earth,
            The Deere,
                the Beare,
                        &c
And &c is the most important gods you missed. For they
were the Manitous, they dwell in you at different times.
                                        If they choose.

3: AUGURY

The blood does not flow from a red vein
as Lawrence through Cooper had it,
and it does not flow from a pale, beautiful
white vein, as Wyndham Lewis had it, and it does not
flow from a black vein as Malcolm X would
have it, the blood does not flow at all.
The land is stained, and it is true
it is stained black, because black is active,
red, the first color of that stain, before black
has washed out and sunk into the ground
and now comes up secret, inward, resistance
where Lawrence was perceptive,

and the white parades, Sousa, where Lewis
with his pale mystic articulation was perceptive
being blind to the throb of black,
but it is all stain, not flow,
black has a gloss, black must have white
black dies without white, Mao is too asiatic
and pure, he can not see across
either the largest land or the largest
water mass he is surrounded by, purity is
his world, business, the chinese business man,
the chinese gambler, the chinese fucker, they
do it, quickly, many many offspring, mass
mass the morass of being working blending, mass
they have no stain, america is stain, the stain
of the west, black and white will blend, obscure
the edge, we shall all fuck that edge away eventually
we so desire each other, the red is oriental, lost
in his most recent place, black and white are the new
camerado—enemies hanging together in every room
in every gutter and A-bomb site every cheap hotel
every penthouse, in the mines on the plains and in
the pumping heart-cornfields of america, every thing
in america is american to a virus, blood spilling
the german blood will not spill, nor the pole
nor the mexican, not italian, not the old previously spilled
no one white kind with the black
                              RED
                  will return
                                    to the East, via the west
        on a landbridge rebuilt
                        past Diomedes
where they will run cattle or spanish horses across siberia
the last of the primitive people in the world

        who can go home

POSTSCRIPT:
"How do you think it feels
When you are speed-ing & lonely"

The caravan wound. Past the pinto bean capital
of the world and mesa verde.
Bitterly cold were the nights.
The journeymen slept in the lots of filling stations
and there were the interrupting lights
of semis all night long as those beasts
crept past or drew up to rest their motors
or roared on.

A modern group in cars.
They travelled north at an angle
and the tired engines whirred
more so the rear plant of the nazi car
from the strain of the great
american desert. Past places
they went, like only mormons
and in Green River
they had coffee and talked to an old woman
whose inconsistency was radical
so demented was she
by the isolation of the spot and the terrible dry winds
that blow down upon south Utah.
and what she had to ward them off
were not the slow dreams of indians
but a pool table and a rack of cold sandwiches.

The beer was cold
The four sat and drank.
Hot, the climate was tolerable only
within the confines of bars or on
the open stretches of road at mad speed
or at night when the bitter cold sat over the southern
Colorado cliffs.

In the bitterness of the great desert
they tried to get comfortable in car seats.

Utterly left behind was
a mixed past, of friends and a comfortable house.

They felt sorry for themselves perhaps
for no real reason, there had never
been in their baggage more than a few stars
and a couple of moons, you've seen their surfaces
in pictures.
They came finally to the brick façade
of salt lake & much beyond. A year later
those who remained celebrated—
almost as an afterthought, and remembered
that day it snowed when they left,
September 1st . . . now it is October
and winter has not yet sent her punitive expedition.
Warm days. It is afternoon. The leaves
come and go in the Alberta wind sliding down
across our country
and they sit still facing the north slopes
of the mountains, the remnant of a Southern Idea
in their minds.

IDAHO OUT

For Hettie and Roi

> *"The thing to be known is the natural
> landscape. It becomes known through
> the totality of its forms."*— CARL O. SAUER

1
Since 1925 there are now no
negative areas he has ignored
the poles have been strung for our time together
and his hand is in the air as well

areal is hopefully Ariel

So black & red simplot fertilizer smoke

drifts its excremental way
down the bottle of our
valley
toward the narrowing
end

coming into the portneuf gap
where its base aspects . . .
a large cork could be placed
but which proceeding from inkom

                             or toward

past the low rooves
of sheep's sheds the slope
gains rough brusque edges
and you are in it more quickly
than its known forms allow

    or the approach from
the contrary side of the valley
there is a total journal
with the eyes
and the full gap stands
as the grand gate from our
place
to utah bad lands and
thus down
to those sullen valleys
of men who have apparently
accepted all of the vital
factor of their time
not including humanity.

    And not to go too far with them
they were the first white flour makers

            they jealously
keep that form and turn the sides

of the citizens' hills into square documents
of their timid endeavor. The only
hard thing they had was first massacre
and then brickwork
not propaedeutic to a life of grand design
wherein *all* men fit
                    but something
for all its pleasure of built surface
and logic of substances as
the appeal of habitat
    for salt lake downtown is
    not ugly,
    but to a life of petty retreat
    before such small concourses
    as smoking, drinking, and other less
    obvious but
    justly necessary bodily needs
    not including breeding which in their hands
    is purposive.

From this valley
there is no leaving by laterals.
Even george goodhart,
a conventional man, as all
good hearts are
knew, with a horse
and access crosswise
to creekheads
the starving indian women could be fed
with surplus deer.

Who was the pioneer boy who died in a rest home
and was a new local, i.e.,
there is implied evidence
he never heard the cry of the pawnee
in his territory.
Which, it is said in the human
ecology term
is to be a hick, howsoever travelled. And
while we are at it it is best said here:

The mark of the pre-communication
westerner
travelled in local segments
along a line of time
utterly sequestered
thus his stupidity required the services
of at least one of his saddle bags
and, in the meantime
his indian friends
signalled one another over his head
as he passed on his businesslike way
in the depressions
between them, in long shadows
they looking deaf and dumb, moving fingers
on the slight rounds
of nebraskan hills.

Of a verge

of the land North
and an afternoon is no good
there is the width of the funnel rim
and sad people for all their smiles
do scurry and sing across its mouth
and there are no archipelagoes of real laughter

in alameda
and no really wild people save stiff
inhibited criminals.

So when gay youth was yours
in those other smaller towns on the peneplain
of central america and the jerseys
the white legs of girls stand truly by stoplights
and Edward Hopper truly did stop painting
all those years. But we stray
we strays, as we always do
and those mercies always wanted

an endless price, our jazz came

from the same hip shops we walked past
the truly, is no sense speaking of universes,
hanging from that hook

        I had in mind the sweet shop
something so simple as main street
and I'll be around.

But I was escorting you out of Pocatello,
sort of north.
Perhaps past that physiographic
menace the arco desert and
what's there
of the leakage of newclear seance

              to Lemhi
again a mormon nomenclature
where plaques to the journey of Lewis & Clark
but the rises across the too
tilted floors of that corridor
at high point the birch
and then toward North Fork
you must take that
other drainage where yes
the opposites are so sheer
and the fineness of what growth
there is that lifting
             following
of line, the forever bush
and its thin colored sentinelling
of those streams
           as North Fork comes on
on the banks of the magnificent salmon
we come smack up on a marvelous beauty from Chi.

    Who has
a creaky cheap pooltable
to pass the winter with
and the innocent loudmouthed handsome
boys who inhabit the

winter there. The remarkably quiet winter
there,
all alone where the salmon forks.
It is so far away but never long ago.
You may be sure Hudson.
And
She said
shaking her dark hair
she used to work at arco
and knew the fastest way
from salmon to idaho falls—
you may be sure
and in a car

         or anywhere,

she was a walking invitation
to a lovely party
her body was that tactile to the eye
or what I meant
she is part
of the morphology
the last distant place of idaho north,
already in effect Montana.
Thus, roughly free,
to bring in relative terms.
Her husband, though it
makes no difference,
had sideburns, wore
a kind of abstract spats
wore loose modern beltless pants
and moved with that accord to the earth
I deal with
but only the heavy people
are with.
    They are "the pragmatic 'and'
the always unequated remnant"

2
My desire is to be
a classical poet
my gods have been men . . .
and women.
I renew my demand
that presidents and chairmen everywhere
be moved to a quarantine outside the earth
somewhere,
as we travel northward. My
peculiar route is across
the lost trail pass past
in the dark draws somewhere
my north fork beauty's husband's
dammed up small dribbling creek

fetching a promising lake (she showed
me the pictures) a too good to be true
scheme she explained to me,
to draw fishermen with hats on
from everywhere
they wanted to come from.
One of the few ventures I've
given my blessing . . . she
would look nice rich.

3
We were hauling . . .
furniture. To Missoula.
We stopped in the biting
star lit air often to have
a beer and stretch our legs.

My son rode with me
and was delighted that a state
so civilized as Montana
could exist, where the people,
and no matter how small

the town,
and how disconnected in
the mountain trails,
could be so welcoming to a lad,
far from the prescribed ages
of idaho where they chase that
young population out, into
the frosty air. There is
an incredible but true fear
of the trespassing there of such
patently harmless people aged 13.

But not to go too much into
that ethnic shit, because
this is geographic business
already, in the bitteroot
there sat snow on the tallest
peaks and that moisture factor
caused trees now gliding by
from one minor drainage
to another until we came
to the great bitterroot
proper and the cottonwoods
and feather honey locusts
lining its rushing edges.
Once, when I was going the other way
in august,
a lemhi rancher
told me the soil content
of the bitterroot was of
such a makeup that the cows
got skinnier whereas
in the lemhi, you know
the rest, although of course
the lemhi is dry. It's
like a boring popular song
all by himself he'd love
to rest his weary head
on somebody else's shoulder
as he grows older.

From Florence to Missoula
is a very pragmatic distance
And florence is the singularity
Montana has, one is so drunk
by that time. Fort Benton,
to your right, across stretches
of the cuts of the Blackfoot, through
Bowman's Corner, no
the sky

       is not

bigger in Montana. When
for instance you come
from Williston
there seems at the border a change
but it is only because man has
built a tavern there
and proclaims himself of service
at a point in time, very much,
and space is continuous from Superior
to Kalispell. And indeed

That is what the dirtiest
of human proportions are built on
service by men there before you

could have possibly come
and you never can.

But if men can live in Moab
that itself is proof nature
is on the run and seeding very badly
and that environmentalism, old word,
is truly dead.

4
So he goes anywhere apparently
anywhere and space is muddied
with his tracks

for ore he is only after,
after ore.
He is the most regretful factor
in a too minuscule cosmic
the universe it turns out your neighbors are

The least obnoxious of all
the radiating circles bring
grossnesses
that are of the strength of bad dreams.

5
Let me remind you we were in Florence
Montana.
Where the Bitterroot is thick
past Hamilton, a farm machinery
nexus
for all that unnutritious hay
and in florence we stop.

Everyone gets out of the trucks
and stretching & yawning moves
through the biting still starlit night
a night covered with jewels
and the trucks' radiators begin
to creak and snap in their cooling off.

We shiver. Each limbjoint
creaks and shudders and we talk
in chatters of the past road, of the failing
head lights on the mountain road—and in
we go.

        A wildly built girl
brushes past us
as we enter. Inside
it is light, a funny disinherited place
of concrete block. The fat woman
bartender,

has an easy smile as we head for the fireplace
in the rear and as we go by the box is putting out
some rock and twist, and on the table
by the fireplace there are canned things, string beans
and corn, and she brings us the beer.

Florence. It is hardly a place.
To twist it, it is a wide spot
in the valley. The air is cold. The fire
burns into our backs while we sit on the hearth.
The girl of the not quite
believable frame
returns, and her boyfriend is pulled
by the vertically rhythmic tips of her fingers
reluctantly off the stool,
but he can't
he, the conservative under riding buttress
of our planet can't, he has been drinking beer
while she, too young for a public place
has been pulling a bottle apart in the car.

So there you are. She is
as ripe and bursting as that
biblical pomegranate.
She bleeds spore in her
undetachable black pants
and, not to make it seem too good
or even too remote
or too unlikely near
she has that
kind of generous smile
offset by a daring and hostile look
again, I must insist, her hair
was black, the color of hostile sex
the lightest people, for all
their odd beauty,
are a losing game.

. . . I can't leave her.
Her mother was with her.

She, in the tavern, in Florence
was ready,
with all her jukeboxbody
and her trips to the car
to the bottle.
There are many starry nights thus occupied
while the planet, indifferent, rattles on
like the boxcars on its skin
and when moments like that transpire
they with all good hope begin again somewhere
She made many trips to the car that night . . .
an unmatchable showoff
with her eyes
and other accomplishments.

6
And onward
bless us, there are no eyes
in Missoula, only things, the new
bridge across Clark Fork
there is civilization again,
a mahogany bar
                    and tickertape

baseball, and the men are men,
but there are no eyes
in Missoula
like in little orphan annie and is?
the sky bigger there?

        The sky disdains
to be thus associated and treacherous cowboys
who drive cars live there.
Say the purity of blue over Houston
that unwholesome place
is prettier
and the graininess over Michoacan is moodier
and I have been to wyoming.

7
The trip back sadly as all trips
back are
          dull
and I did
see the old bartender woman of florence
this time in her restaurant part 50 yards
away from the tavern between which
she ran apparently with the speed
of some sort of stout gazelle
but not the broad with the fabulatory build.
She that day was probably off in an office somewhere.
Pity daytime lives.

But everyone was tired. We had unloaded
the furniture, early the next morning
and before the bite of the sun quelled the bite
of the stars we left, going the long, time consuming
way
south. Sober business.
The Beauty of North Fork was there as she will be
till she dies sometime
(and by the way she runs a tavern)
Thence to salmon and across the narrow bridge
and out
into the lemhi. I say
if it weren't for the distances
and for the trees & creeks I would
go mad, o yes, land, that one forces
a secondary interest in, vanishes
as a force as you drive onward.
This is only obvious.
This is only some of the times we spend.
You go through it as though it were
a planet of cotton wadding . . . and love
its parts as you do the parts of a woman
whose relations with earth are more established
than your own.

But of physical entirety
there is no need to elaborate, one has
one's foot
on the ground, which is the saying
of all common and communicable pleasures
and my arm around your shoulder is the proof of that.
But I am ashamed of my country
that, not as areal reality, but as act
it shames me to be a citizen in
the land where I grew up. The very air chills
your bones, the very ungraciousness of its replies
and the pressures of its not replying
embarrass my presence here. God knows
we do what we can to live.
But the intimidations thrown at us
in the spurious forms they have learned truth
can take, in a time which should have been
plenty and engaging of the best that each man,
if he were encouraged to be even that, and
not slapped in the face as stupid, cut off
from all other peoples to make him hygienic of
views not viable to this soil, which is no more
sacred I tell you than any other the earth
has to offer, for she in her roundness has kept
an accord with her movements great time has not yet
seen aberrant. Mice crawling on a moving body?
can they, may they really offset great movement?

The very air,
if you are awake, can chill your bones
and there is little enough of beauty
finally scratched for. It is not
the end pursuit of my countrymen
that they be great
in a great line of men.
An occasional woman, won't,
though I wish she could,
justify a continent. In the parliaments
of minuscule places she is there

120

and gives them substance,
as in Florence, and North Fork
for she was gracious as leaders
are now not and I begin to believe after all
these years there *is* an aristocracy
of place and event and person
and as I sit here above this valley
I sought to involve you with
and take you out on a trip
that had no point, there remains Montana
        and it is nice. But not infallible.
The sky is a hoax.
And was meant,
once suggested,
to catch your eye. The eye
can be arbitrary,
but its subject matter cannot.
Thus the beauty of some women.
And from Williston
along the grand missourian length
of the upper plains you go, then the Milk
to Havre
that incredible distance once along a route
all those clamorous men
took . . . they now grow things there not horticultural
only storageable, things of less importance
than fur
for furs then were never stockpiled, it would
hurt the hair,
                    that Astor,
he'd never have done it.

And yes Fort Benton is lovely
and quiet, I would gladly give it as a gift
to a friend, and with pride, a place of marked
indolence, where the river closes, a gift
of marked indifference, if it were mine.
If the broad grass park were mine
between the river and the town

121

and to the quick rise behind.
And then up to the median altitude of Montana
Sugar beets and sheep and cattle.

Where the normal spaces
are the stretches of Wyoming
and north Dakota, Idaho
is cut
by an elbow
of mountain that swings
down, thus she is
cut off by geologies she says
I'm sure
are natural
but it is truly the West
as no other place,
ruined by an ambition and religion
cut, by a cowboy use of her nearly virgin self

        unannealed
by a real placement
                this,

this
is the birthplace
of Mr. Pound
and Hemingway in his own mouth
chose to put a shotgun.

SIX VIEWS FROM THE SAME WINDOW
OF THE NORTHSIDE GROCERY

(for Helene on Washington's birthday)

1

Saturday afternoon. The hill is a reminder
with its slope of a counterpart outside
Sedro Woolley—wooded second growth there
snow and the black scars of juniper here.
The glass shines with the land beyond
red freight cars and the vast house of shops.

2

We occupy red enameled chairs
in the backroom, drink beer and eat greek
cheese and olives, white salt of the cheese
black salt of the shrivelled olive spit
into the ash tray. Beyond the old pink front
the red green stripes of the awning sway in the breeze
of these last days of February. All the panes
remarkable of clarity, an uncle sam kite
writhes up from the hands of the black boy
the rattle of its paper cannot be heard.

3

Goat cheese and greek olives. The owner
is sullen and friendly, he calls the black women sister
they come and go inside his grocery, one thing at a time
it does not pretend to be a small supermarket.
Cold air, clean glass. We rest and watch.
The occasion for this excursion is in the selected strings
of a life gone terribly lonely. It will be a march.
A frail cloud moves with silence into the window.
No sound in the store. No bell on the door.

4
The dark children fly their kite—
we share a common exile—they run
I stay here in the woven light
of a backroom.
It is pointless to make verse of this fibre. I could write
all the names of my absent friends
on the window in black
and the light would grow less
and then lesser
and I would sit motionless
on the dark side of my thought
I would sit in the deep shade of my yearning
I would have supplied me the proper nouns
of my darkness.

5
And my lady looks from the same window, over
one yard altogether away, another picture
of the world, white house isolated, a lost railroad
building, this vast change rung with the same air
and we are, by the same air, a rest of those
measures of wood, of the same kite, cans bounded
by trash she has in her view, and poles
of loosely hung wire, some power lost altogether
back of the glass as the trembling portrait
of uncle sam, of all the continuing weirdness
in the ennui of the falling sun, and I stare at her
and her lips part very little, slow and pleasantly
vagrant talk, the measures are the stillnesses
made various by the code of friends' names, those nouns
drop like greek olives from our fingers, and the pits
are in a real way the crashing verbs of
a mistaken local rapport. Be patient
and give me your hand, there is something of a beginning
everywhere, this is a new part of town.

6

There is a part of the world over your shoulder
can't be seen in a window and can't be pulled
through the holes in one's eyes yet a fixture
of some boundaries is a small cure haphazardly grasped
or torn loose from a confused day, a tiresomeness
arrived with a permanent smile hand outstretched
I love you now more than ever and stand waving my arms
at the edge of a swarm of self breeding considerations
to say it, the mailbox, that post, is sought out
by both of us a triangulation of what we share
as elsewhere,
it is a twin exile, the small town's portion
of futility, the self mockery with an interchangeable tire
that makes us dare what we are. Thus a window
is that seemingly clear opening our tested knowledges
pass through and the world shakes not at all
before the weight of our appointments, you will
and would be part of the new hemisphere
until it dies of the same old loosely wrought manifestoes.
All those sounds from the broken washing machine
are trying to tell you something sweetheart don't laugh
one day it will speak and not stop
all things have an insistence of their own.

DAFFODIL SONG

The horns of yellow

on this plain resound
and the twist on the air
of their brilliance
Say where
say where I will find
a love
or an arabesque
of such rash fortune.

SONG

my wife is lovely
my children are fair
she puts color on her lips
in front of the mirror
there is stillness everywhere
my hand is on her shoulder
we are leaving the house
the sun is in her hair
and since october
it has grown darker
there is frost in the air
I am unwise
to think of her as there
those parts of her I adore
are here
the years have gone by
everywhere
now our house is near

alongside other houses
we laugh, sometimes,
sometimes we construct
a single blue tear

LOVE SONG

for Lucia

Captured, her beauty
would not leave her
thus inclined by the railing
she never lifted her head
from the waters
a blue gull drifts
     she moves from the rapture
of the ascending fog.
Lost in the moving passengers
she left the ship
and entered the city.

LOVE SONG

for Cathy

Out of the north branch of the river
out of the foam of it running
runs my desire
so the fish fall never ending
continually forward
and she stays eternally there
and indolent winter stars
are in her eyes
     indolent as she resides
all seasons by the fork
of my desire.

A VAGUE LOVE

The Bannocks stand by the box
they sway to the music.
A California truck driver
in with a load of pianos
shoots pool.

Their women
are not beautiful
they are not

but their eyes
have deep corridors in them
of brown hills of pain and
indecision and under every
searching lash

a question no man, not
even their own
can answer.

Where is the *deer?*
That is not the question.

tic tok, stop de clock.
sings Fats Domino.

We all stand swaying.
it's someone's turn to shoot.

ANOTHER VAGUE LOVE

Down 5th it is cold
yes the dry air is filled

with pieces of dust
they cut the eye as would a file.

Driven along, every day
toward center
this is a town
of vague love

And what you see if you can
is the truth:

SONG

Oh Gods of my disembarked soul this is sad
a merriment of unteachable waywordness
I tell you the gleaming eye
is a mirror of
                    the green hills
where love struggles
                    against the drought
in the desert
in the spring
in the quickness
of the fresh bush
          over the cove.

A WILD BLUE, YONDER

Let me say
we had a canary
who rode to Idaho
with Bob Creeley

swinging in the cage
on the seat beside him

Sadly in the last of March
I opened our door
and the bird flew out before me
but that was hours ago

A very nice bird,
liked Syeeda's song flute
and returned always to the cage
to roost, and had taken
to a picture of that man
on our shelf, which we then put
in the window facing out

                              to summon it
Helene saw out the window
a bright blue
bird in the sage
and felt better and
then we gave it up.

IN THE SHADOW

a dim light shines. The city
is reflected on the overcast
when our conveyance comes
in. Late September. Cool.

She rises just another move
in the dark just another
month another moist point
on my dead journey.

Her mouth I never saw
nor the surprise of
her busy limbs, yes her
eyes strayed.

It was late September and
cool air pale shadows held sunset
in their traces.
She left in a car, the dust grew.

SONG

If the world
or a life
or all of this
love,
all the pleasures
we do not sow
and those we do
love,
sometime end.

                    If any of this
end
      we will know
what we knew to be in
a vacancy
of dreams
of costly motion
temporary cities
and our happy faces
where we were determined
as some blunt nosed dog
            permitted exercise
from tree
      to tree
on the public concern

131

A SONG

There is a blue sky
over the flower, there is
a green sea beneath
yet there is no bliss
along my way now . . .

In the casual flight of this day
there is a yellow flower edged
in blue
there is a sky filled with snow
and along my way there few bright calls
of spring, there is hardly a chance
there are ahead no tricks
to turn a season, all friends
are sober.

I have a dark blue sky
inside my head, ah,
there is a flower here
and there, and yes, believe
I'll miss this time, sometime,
these old cold mountains
these cold blue hills
sometime.

THE EXPLANATION

There was a dark interior
where I waited and there
were dark odors dark music. All my days

pressed flat, float
off
in the breeze.

The sky over the southern arc is leaden,
rain, falling or not
running in the gutters
or not, is rare here.

We left with dexterity but desperation
a place we could no longer abide
and all explanations now seem
unfit, unfit.
The long sought ease

a hand on a curved hip
was part of other lives
and offered no explanation and got
a ready stare
                    so falteringly
to the wall I went
and they said My My
and shook their heads.

CHRONICLE

It is January 12
and midwinter, the great dipper
stands on its handle in the sky
over pocatello.
The air, a presence
around the body when I go out
the door to relieve myself
is well below zero.

133

Yes it is well below.
This land is well
below, say shoot it, longitude
and latitude, yet it stings
like the Yukon, and standing,
to get back to that,
I thumb my nose several times
at the city below, it is midnight
and the lights are stationary
through the cool absent fog.

Inside Fred plays his cello
and that air sings thereby.
I run my fingers through my hair.
Here, all around, is
the world, out
on points, on the horizon are
friends close and far gone.
With the tautness of those
chorded strings bind them
together,
this air will kill us all
ere long.

SONG

So we somewhat stagger together
down the street, heads down
smiling and not smiling
she making her ceaseless prattle
and laughter
                she is the goddess
who leads us after a worried pedestrian
or a hapless dog, and I go

always it's true wrapped in a cloud
a press of obscurity that keeps me
in a small car of priority
a propriety
            of attention
        and not missing any part of it
she is that tactile
on the street,
against my side, taking us
around the circumference of desire

                        oh stars be bright!
in the forecast of your grand moments
and when the terror and pestilence
you will surely drive with a stake into my heart
is there
let us have been
for a while
                    in a superior conjunction
                    back of the sun.

SONG

Christ of the sparrows Help me!
    the soot falls
        along the street
    into the alleys.
december.

and sometimes
    its rain falls
        along pocatello's streets
    into its alleys
    along its black diesel thruways

135

There is no far away place
could satisfy
there is no forlorn bird
could outdistance my desire.
When the vacation
of my heart is that complete
the pain of this
particular moment
is unbearable. The sun
strikes my book laden table
my room is my skull
I could have you tell me
this pain behind my eyes will soon be gone
I could listen, I could die
seized by a foolishly contrived misunderstanding

or listlessly watch
        the two single
figures bent
and in the rags of careful hesitation
feel their way along the sidewalk
past my window
old men
leave a city already made lonely
by the outcast words of pointless conversation
        go,
along the intolerably windy highway west of here.

    And mind us
there were no marks of the bruise of friends
there aren't any traces of that turmoil, you stay
as you were, there were
a few headlong pitches onto the ground
a torn shoulder to remember
a few unhappy nights.
drunk with the high necessity to talk
fast and loud in crowded bars
And then, in the street
to spit silently out

the cheap guilt
and all the casual half meant and self aware
inward chastisement
a petty reward for myself, like saving a nickel
and insisting even with a smile
it was *my* life I lived
the suspicious terror I'd turned around
too many times to keep track
I said you said I said You said I said.

PARLOR CAR BEER

They look coach, in the morning
pants wrinkled.
And I *am* coach, CHICAGO spelled out
across my front teeth.
Don't want to be sleeper.

    They
look sleeper
coming in from the other end, the
dirty & tired
have a beer
with the rested & clean.

    Get this:
we talked of the all England
ice skating championships, 1959

    How
some skills pass the understanding
of the uninitiated
right in the middle of Nebraska

POEM IN FIVE PARTS

1
Van goghs boats
sat on the beach
as I sit here
good lord as I sit here

and van goghs boats
are upturned
the bows set east
as I do

and the crosspieces
on the masts
they are strung out
as my arms are

oh were I only
red &
white &
blue

and in the distance
more white as
the sails, the
lonely white
triangulars
are

dim-
inishing

how I am
only
as the distance
goes

blue

2
I love you

3
Februaries
are hard to face
there were trees
this winter possessed
of a grace
they are
white bare
siberian elm
around the corner
in the garden
the cold air
this spring—
will be
    changed
    and obscured
deformed
as I will
a growth
of indetermination
while waiting
out the season

4
I have
certain dreams
at midday
and you are their vintner
at eleven I go
for the mail, a card
a misconcordance
of a letter
on missing, a lapse

of two months
the cement is frigid
beneath my bare feet
it is the end of january

5
Where are you
Henry James sits
on the table, an increment
of difficult sentences
the same sun shines
   you left without one thought
of me
without one desire
to let me know
or look back
all at once,
              as if suddenly
you ignored one half year
of mutual consent

I am a casual fool
now
I do so regard
the labor
of my own
              careful
peace of mind.

SONG

This afternoon was unholy, the sky
bright mixed with cloud wrath, I read Yeats,
then black, and their land of heart's desire
where beauty has no ebb
                              decay no flood
but joy is wisdom, time
an endless song
                              I kiss you
and the world begins to fade
I kiss you not, the world is not.
I would not give my soul to you yet
the desire inside me burns.
November. The eighteenth was the coldest
this season, encumbered with routine errands
out past the factory
                              black sulphur
and in the dense checks
of its burdensome smoke the intense yellow tanks,
hooded, there sat a smell of weak death

and we pass these days of our isolation
in our rigidly assigned shelters
heads bent in occupation
a couple of pointless daydreamers
smiles lit and thrown into the breeze,

    how artful can love
suffer in the cross streets of this town
marked simply by the clicking railroad
and scratch of the janitor's broom.

DARK CEILING

Broad black scar the valley is
and sunday is
where
        in the wide arc
    the small lights of homes come on
in that trough.

        Burnish my heart
        with this mark

Furnish my soul with the hope
Far away and by a river
In the darkness of a walnut stand.

There
        is
no home, no back.

All is this wrong key, the lark
sings
        but his voice trails off
in the snow. He has not
brought his meadow.
The starling's
  insolent whistle
is the truth here—dark smoke

drifts in from the morning fertilizer factory
and men there return lamely
to work, their disputes not settled.

THIS MARCH AFTERNOON

Pride kept me away.
           Her eyes, indelicate
as they were,
were there nonetheless
           and her eyes guided
me into the recesses of my own
               untrackable
world, oh goddesses
did I like Harpagus crave a future rule
of this world as over the years I grow older?
A bitter clot of time rides in my throat
and Nay once again the Graces say.

SONG: HEAT

               Massive time
the pacific controls our continent
but what controls me is far
less in size than that and far
more burning, oh heat

a continent is my forge
buried deep in the caloric inside
is our relative, the fire
     the twin bellows of love
          cavity of the chest
in the mountain the door
on the lips the red explosion
in the valley the unlit incubator
     sperm of politics flow
            a river

in the ocean of the edges
basins catch us
in the mystic of the spray the return
onto the land again
      the spore of politics
the ringing arrangement of love

SONG: WE SHALL REFRAIN FROM THEM

On the shore of our world
there appeared one day
an unhappy coincidence
of natures born but not meant
for each other. An infernal compliment.

      And no more
was said. No more intended.
There is bred a dark hurt, an intersection
far smaller than time
too brief to exist in space
             of a luminosity
far redder than the red flash
               of the tongue
         of Eve's keen snake
now we are at the tranquil pass in our mountains
all we had expected, all we had
made secure
is routine. The cool valley beyond
is filled with cabbages of persons
in rows to the end of time
their heads are fixed
and it is not that they can't see Icarus
rise in his superb ambition
but they will not, they will not see

trap and they slay
they pretend to know nothing of frivolity
where their whole pleasure is instruction
in that quality.

But they have no gods at all to play with
they have invented *one*, a dull number
and they wave small flags of angry color
in one shrivelled hand, on one stunted arm.

THE SMUG NEVER SILENT GUNS OF THE ENEMY

Their muzzles are at the door.
Did you see them, did he
see them, minutemen
rising out of the silos
A winter wonderland of
the white busy north.
The smug guns, trained on
The whites of their eyes
are grey
            and disputations
of more guns come
into the ear:
    The manipulated price of sugar
    The death of great ladies
    "I'll shoot my second if you'll shoot yours"
    Concentrated insecticides
    (flow like milk in the river
    You will be greeted
    on the outskirts of town
    with a vegetable brush
    and tips on good living

An interview with a turkey farmer
        (gobbling in the background
the news that Bertrand Russell
    is a sick old fool
The seminar ends when the squat madeyed colonel
    announces the way to peace thru war and shoots the moderator

And more corrupted reports follow you out
the door, they implore you to think young
and you do
it is such a pleasure in the sagebrush
in the open saturated air
zipping up your pants
having made more of the latest news
on the new snow.

FORT HALL OBITUARY: A NOTE

        A drinking party
(no war party)

        Sunday morning
        they drank solax
        containing methyl . . .

Fort Hall Indian Police
found Reeta Poonee, 37
dead inside a shack.

        Bigbear passed out
        in a car
        outside the door

they were all watched closely.

(Bigbear taken Bannock County jail
warrant charging disorderliness
checked regularly

But when Deputy John Gouge checked at 7:20 a.m.
there was no more Bigbear . . .

and thus,
          Coroner Justin Juice said
No goddamn autopsy heah into this
heah death! Ah am satisfied they died
          from drinkin.

and Reeta
and Bigbear

          are

MOURNING LETTER, MARCH 29, 1963

No hesitation
          would stay me
from weeping this morning
for the miners of Hazard Kentucky.
          The mine owners'
extortionary skulls
whose eyes are diamonds don't float
down the rivers, as they should,
of the flood

          The miners, cold
starved, driven from work, in
their homes float though and float

on the ribbed ships of their frail
bodies,

Oh, go letter,
keep my own misery close to theirs
associate me with no other honor.

EUGENE DELACROIX SAYS

dated Valmont 10-16
october 1849
the common people
will always be
the majority

they make a mistake
in thinking
that great estates
are useless

But furthermore he says
It is the poor
who benefit most by them

And the profits gained do not
impoverish the rich who
let, them,
take advantage of the little
to be sure
windfalls
which they find on their estates.

Now let us begin again this morning.
The poor.

And the middle class
or anyone might
fence off their approaches
necessity is a naturally
more separable thing
                              than poverty.
In this case the poor were
allowed to gather fuel
on the estates, given them that right
by the republican, fear that word,
government.

Much as today the man bent between the tracks
in Appalachia east kentucky
his malnourished and unemployed fingers
articulating very small pieces of coal indeed
and his children grimly beautiful
because their eyes have been made large
as witnesses
as the lean roll of years and owners
stripped the hills of their former
mountain glamour.
                              Bent in the dim light
of that specific cabin space they had,
those unlucky children, a meal
of various cereal dumped on the market
to make room for vaster crops next year
a thing they couldn't have understood
or that charity is quite often
a device to prevent spoilage,

                              nor were they
ever allowed to consider that the merely farinaceous
will not support the life
of a carnivore. But this is just
the bestiality of the major euphemism
of our day, supplementation.
Retrained they may become garage mechanics
and press the temptation
of match cover education

between their fingers
the rest of their days here in the western hemisphere.
Now, if a fire has to be made
and a supper has to be got, that's not
here nor there, here,
but back of Recife they *wonder* a lot of the time
in Kentucky they do not
in all of Hazard county they do not.
And it is an inevitability that one day
those ugly eyes prolix with beefsteak will be
snatched out, and south america
will have been all along much to their amazement
a specific location not to have been misused
and kentucky will have been a noun
that smouldered like a burning mine
and, I have to add, I hope those satraps
do not wake in time.

SONG: VENCEREMOS

*(for latin america
(for préman sotomayor*

And there will be fresh children once more
in planalto and matto grosso
green mansions for their houses
along the orinoco
        take away the oil
        it is not to anoint their heads
        take away the cannon
        and the saber from the paunch belly
        overlaid with crossed colors
        those quaint waddling men
        are the leaden dead toys

                              only their
                       own
                    children
                       caress
            while the great eyed children
            far away in the mountains, out of Quito
            pass thru the crisp evening streets
            of earth towns, where they caress
            the earth, a substance of *majority*
            including the lead of established
            forces,
who can do nothing
            but give us the measures of pain
               which now define us

Take away the boats from the bananas
they are there for the double purpose
to quell insurrection first
and next to make of an equatorial food
a clanging and numerical register in chicago
this is not an industrial comment,
it is not Sandburg's chicago
not how ugly a city you did make
but whitman's fine generosity I want
a specific measure of respect returned for the hand
and the back that bears away the stalk
as a boy, in illinois
peeled away, in amazement, the yellow, brown lined case
                              thicker place
when the arced phenomenon
was first put in his hand
a suggestion and a food, combustion!
keep your fingers from the coffee bush.

                              Nor,
on the meseta Basáltica, or back in town
in Paso de Indios
can the people be permitted
the luxurious image of Peron

and his duly wedded saint
they can be taught to deny
the dictator and his call girl
in the sports car
hide themselves in some corrupt
rooming house country
with a blue coast
and damned clergy

      "memory, mind, and will
        :politics
    "there are men with ideas
    who effect"

Force those men.
be keen to pass beyond all known use
use the grain on a common mountain
for those who are hungry
             treat hunger
as a ceremony
be quick to pass by condition
and the persuasion of mere number
     teach the parrot, who rises
           in the sunset
       a cloud
        to sing,
destroy
     all talking parrots
  I ask you
     make for the
         altar
    of your imaginations
    some sign   Keep
    the small clerks of God from your precinct
be not a world, and therefore halt
before the incursions of general infection
       from a stronger world,
   dance,
        and in your side stepping

                    the spirit
                 will tell where.

THE SENSE COMES OVER ME,
AND THE WANING LIGHT OF MAN
BY THE 1ST NATIONAL BANK

        My stepfather stood on the corner
by the national bank, quiet

                    the hot lights
nights moved on
between those week periods
                    the old men
spat, they seemed possessed of stronger points
a willingness to jut from their foreheads
not articulation but a world of determination and only
that, an insistence, a manifestation of the bottom jaw
then, as now, the most stupidly local preoccupation,
                                        you think
this is abstract,
               nigger no, don't
and there weren't. Not there, of course, we were
                                    alone
and it could be said there were questions unformed
for the lapse of any plausible answer, the walnut dropped
literally onto the ground in the woods
and rotted there through the year, and the people cried
out in their ineffectual way for white flour and pork,
canned peaches my aunt brought once was a ceremony
                                        I almost
waited under the table.
                    The afternoons. So Do you
think to think of love? Or weld
that affair

                    153

with the heat of ancient transplanted tassels,
the relief of mystically rough elements
                                    The dead watch
of the sun,
the unyielding severity of a farmer feeding pigs
the routine collection of mud
mixed with the sharp green smell of excrement on their boots
old times gone over
                    save us
from the anterooms of the moral what
the shiftless which everyone wore, blue jackets
overalls, an unspoken sign in the starch, laundry
was very much, as now, a form of calculation, land
                                        and starch,
this is no judgement, this is
the weight of dissimilar things bound together
by a strictly regulated common deprivation
the low and the high, no middle, held in a smiling equilibrium
you may eat only the shit I give you. One could not
comprehend. . . Under a mulberry tree the road was purple
with their running from their farms into town. Passing
at night on the black road in the car I marked the passing
over those spots under those boughs. It meant nothing, it
could mean nothing, one would not have mentioned it. Abandoned
the trees were like my youth. It was a stain of assurance
I preferred to the cant on the bank steps but an utterly sad
and contemptible inability to insist on the stain of reality
and a woe of that lowly order became my sign and weight in that
        land.
            I became that land and wandered out of it.
Sharp
        and keen with the fever
this thrill of spring in the Lord's prayer
which I carried and still love as a vague solace
I carry, confused
                    that ceaseless speculation over
the ways of love
into the darker borders

154

of my wounded middle years,
                              a practical self-pity

    There was a girl
    who was a resolution
    with whom I walked the empty streets
    and climbed the watertower for one night
    to show off, she standing a white spot of summer
    on the ground, and looked out I did
    over the lights of a realm I thought grander than
    and any of it, altogether, was very little, and when
    the pictographic scratches in the silver paint told me
    as I walked around
    the cat-walk expression of what had happened in the 1930's
    men vomiting from hunger
    on the thin sidewalk below, a lonely mason
    with his business ring on, but beyond,
    in the little shoe repair shops the men,
    part of a hopeless vigilante, exhaling the slow mustard gas
    of World War I. My mother, moving slowly in a grim kitchen
    and my stepfather moving slowly down the green rows of corn
    these are my unruined and damned hieroglyphs.
                              Because they form
the message of men stooping down
in my native land, and father an entire conglomerate
of need and wasted vision. All the children
were taught the pledge of Allegiance, and the land was pledged
to private use, the walnut dropped in the autumn on the ground
green, and lay black in the dead grass in the spring.

    there they do lie, the principal
residue of my past, and the past
of my gutless generation, nineteen year olds
invaded the white house today, a screen
was put up to shield the nervous exit
of Ladybird, they sang and refused to move,
she split and I felt it possible again
at the end of a very long winter

to be a less schizophrenic american, a little
of the pus was spooned out of my brain, I gave
an arbitrary grade to a backward black girl
I remembered to spit on the sidewalk
when I thought of the first 35 hundred marines
who landed in Vietnam yesterday. I spoke of
President Johnson as the logical extension of
Increase Mather, my heart, like theirs,
a "civit box of sin" and late in the afternoon
explained *Metamorphosis,* and Kafka as a product
of a hung up family, and a hung up people,
bringing forward, inching nearer
the perpetuality of the lives we lead on the edge
of the great american desert where you certainly
do not
want to be buried but buried you are, the horizons
recede before you, they are busy with the presentations,
that remote we are, of the tilting planes of escape
. . . which are: the speculation of what we might do,
         an *imagination* of the geometry
         of our location
         the problem of the potato
         stamped to identify its place of origin,
         that, for one of the poorest of foods

No one
has loved the west I came into, this is not
a Shulamite maiden, nor does anyone care to whisper
this far into our ear, the allegory does not exist, the marriage
will not come who would marry Simplot or Anaconda
I warn you world of good intention the birth of Mohammed
will be fought in this neck of the cut-off world
and moved on, any new blood will
turn to an unnumberable plasma
we could still walk into the banks
and demand the money, but the usual sadness
—we have been preceded, there is
nothing so lame and halt as lateness

SONG: RITUAL PARTY IN AN ALLEY

The young teach
        the young
    in almost *all*
almost all
                societies
    the old men teach
    and the novice is put under
            a blanket
            afraid to look
        while the old men around the fire
                        prepare
            the sheathblade
        a stone before steel
        and before stone
        they rent off
                    with their teeth
            the pubertal cover
            the blanket of the phallus

    thus ushered toward the majority
        a new sheath of clay for the penis wound
        (in the States that means drink

        and drink, the young
        are drunk into it, deserted

    the young teach
            themselves, no poultice for the wound
                    they are obviously
                    inturned, in spite
                their whistles
                are so tuned
                into broods

            they go into broods
            always one, always many

to be left at the edge
with the old men

to join the ranks
of the old men, every one of them
too late, in their blue suits

the medicine dirt of the earth
showered from them
their world is ugly
with infection

A LUXURIOUS JUNGLE IN WHICH

They are the police
the flowers
in a deep jungle too rife to transgress
the bars, believe me, grow
as any vegetation, look say the substantial voices
of any place and you do, the details of our terror
are that
distracting
because it is your game they
seek to persuade you to play.
the irony Hawthorne caught
the large mystic gesture Melville made
inside an utter disregard and disdain
for the local.

The flowers grow in jail. The penetration
of light, the atmosphere of possibility,
and don't call that abstract, call that a man and woman
hanging their heads by a single artery, call that what
the thread of life is, not what instead it might be

call that garden History, do not call it eden
an allegorical tale based on certain unlikely presumptions.

SONG: EUROPA

Red wine will flow
sadly past your lips, and leave
with fullness their parting
october is orange
with desolation
the mountains are abandoned
each winter sunset
to those cruel marks of red
or whole lines of remote ranges
lit of desire for you as they recede
                              toward oregon

Nothing will happen.
The brutality of your frankness
has come to me
inches at a time,
and so slowly the pain marches
through the veins of my soul
with the heavy step of a migrating herd
tramping out the vintage
Evening is
              that closing part
of you I sometimes hum as a song to myself
looking down the street through my fingers
through the wreath of myrtle
                        with which you have embellished
                              my horns

159

I call
with the thick weight
in my throat
over your terrain
                    O she is a small settlement, there
she is an atmosphere
and we are above it all
under her white gown
                    and against my bare shoulder
snow flakes fall
        a slight scent of ginger
    fresh in the wind
of our trip to Knossos

FOR THE NEW UNION DEAD IN ALABAMA

The Rose of Sharon
        I lost in the tortured night
of this banished place
    the phrase
        and the rose
        from wandering
away, down the lanes
    in all their abstract directions
    a worry about the peninsula
of the east,
            and the grim territories
                of the west
            here in the raw greed
        of the frontier my soul can find
    no well of clear water
        it is pressed
    as a layer
        between unreadable concerns,

160

a true sandwich, a true
grave, like a performance
in an utterly removed theater
is a grave, the unreachable action makes
a crypt
of distance,
a rose of immense beauty
to yearn for.
the cutting of it
cutting off the world
the thorn however
remains, in the desert
in the throat of our national hypocrisy
strewn we are along all the pathways
of our exclusively gelding mentality
we stride in
our gelding culture.
oh rose
of priceless beauty
refrain from our shores
suffocate the thin isthmus
of our mean land.
cast us back
into isolation

THE WORLD BOX-SCORE CUP OF 1966

Hello Fans !   Welcome to the opening of the World Cup
this shld be an exciting game today we have everyone
in the World here today. Just looking down over the
crowd here I see many of the famous celebrities who
have travelled or come in some other way to be here
this afternoon to *see* and be a part of this great
contest between the best fed players from the many
free countries representing the *entire* free world
and then we have the skinny pot—and I mean that
word straight bellied players from all the aggressive,
tenacious countries fans all over the world have learned
to respect because of the fighting spirit these unfortunate
players have on more than one occasion displayed, as for
the *many* celebrities who I wld be inclined to say are
almost legion we'll get to them from time to time
during the breaks in the game here this balmy fine,
completely atypical anglo-american afternoon, the
English team completely trained by that great great
competitor Deck Helms one of the *many* top flight
prototypes here this afternoon, at this *delicious*

FIRST QUARTER

. . . ulations versus the Havenots
Havenots runnin after the ball they almost
woops fans like you aint gonna believe this
but referee America just stepped in an took
the ball
          and gives it
that's right I believe yes he does he gives it
to, yes actually that's right he does give it
to Al Capp, visiting underdeveloped captain
of the England team here this very windy afternoon
and actually now that we do have a break
and some philipino players of the Havenot team

162

have been vanished to vietnam, the penalty
under american rules for trying to get the ball,
I think I'll just turn to Kenneth Tynan who's here
in the box with me this very cold, blustery
I might even say, windy, afternoon, and can you
just tell the audience here this afternoon, Ken
this cold windy and as I said blustery afternoon
a little about the flik you're making Called Andy Capp
meets Al Capp, you're actually shooting some of it
right here this afternoon aren't you, as I've said
this windy, cold, even blustery, but extremely exciting
afternoon here between the Haves, represented by England
and the Havenots, represented by everybody,
all those poor not-with-it players without shirts
by the way Ken just before you answer that I
would like to comment on the way the good people
who made all this possible got around just one
of the many difficult technical problems of bringing us
this great show in the way they PAINTED the numbers
on the Havenot players *bare backs* as I understand
after a quick consultation it was decided to use
whitewash instead of permanent paint when it was
Pointed Out by one american adviser that statistics
showed not one of the Havenot players
would be alive for next years playoff isn't that
an Interesting Sidelight here this afternoon at this
great playoff
between the Haves and the Havenots look at those resourceful fans
they're burning a member of the Havenot team
down by the goal post just to our right here on this
Blustery, chilly, very windy afternoon I'm sorry
there's no more time Kenneth Tynan and as the teams
come back onto the field I'd just like to point out
a few of the many notables here at this wonderful, exciting
world playoff, John Gardner of the washington HEWs
who got his early training under that great Harvard
psychologist H. Al Murray who a few of you fans
may remember ironed all the ambiguities out of *Pierre*

that great novel of Herman Mellville's, and Gardner himself
was of course the man who gave us the New Math, a great
competitor. And of course there's Dean Rusk that veritable
Pandoras box of the international scene and watching the game
with him is Mac Namarra who earned the plaudits of fans
all over the world
when he refused to pronounce Viet Nam
and now the marching band of 500 university poets
is being hustled off the field as the teams prepare
to resume play . . .

SECOND QUARTER

And now play has almost resumed
this afternoon, at Yanqui-go-home Stadium
right at the very edge of wog world
france spain belgium germany, countries like that
are just across the channel here, as we sit here
waiting for the play to take on some spark
in this great, this very great,
this very world league Series

In the meantime I notice our
roving mike has picked up a fan, Ha Ha
a very long haired fan I might add, can't
imagine how he got in here this afternoon
our South African Fun Squad usually kill them
at the box office by setting *fire* to their *hair*
with this special novelty outsize cigarette lighter
kindly donated by the Ronson people, just
a little lethal fun and diversion for all the many
normal people here this afternoon
as they stand in their queues, so before we interview
our guest this is Stern Bill your endless Sportscaster
bringing you all the highlights of your World
                              Playoff, your chance
to see the most undernourished of the underdeveloped
World fall before the terrific onslaught here of the
formidable, I might say invincible IBM selected

Men of Good Will and Good Food from the Major
Christian Nations, and by the way
Russia qualified to play on the Developed side
for the first time in the long history of this series
by buying 500,000 Fiats from Italy and burning
2 of its second rate authors. We're ready to go
thru now with our first interview of this as yet
uneventful 2nd quarter so I'll just switch you
down into the stands, actually they're compounds
on the underdeveloped side, but before I do
I will explain for the benefit of our radio audience,
you people watching TV can see for yourselves
exactly what the problem is, just why we're getting
such a slow start here this afternoon—what
you transistor fans can't see is this Delay
we're having getting the underdeveloped players *onto*
the playing field, or pitch, and the problem
is further complicated by the fact that due

                    to *dissension* or
disagreement among the players of the underdeveloped
squad they have used what little reserves of energy
they had and thus during the 2nd quarter herethisafternoon
they have to be *carried* onto the field by the Developed
reserve, a disgusting thing for our players to
have to do and believe you me they're not liking it
one little bit, the smell from the nearly *dead*
opposition, and I use that term advisedly
must be atrocious, and now that I mention it there is
an interesting note *on* the Underdeveloped team, 90%,
that's over half, of the members have been the victims
of atrocities somewhere in the dark, *barely* understood
scarcely envisaged backward world
                              And now I see we're ready
with the interview, and so, we switch away now
from this *great* but *as yet* actionless contest
and Who do we have here this afternoon
                              You say you're a Trog

165

That's very interesting, I understand from an article
in the *News of the World,* that great competitive newspaper
that the group you call yourself a part of is *holed up*
in caves in the north midlands somewhere, which is by the way
one of the great developed areas of the free world
and which I'd just like to say here, and commend it,
makes possible the decent lives a few people in the Bahamas
those great sunny Islands, I'd even say those Fun Islands
are able, thanks to your great area, to live. Now
there *have* been rumors that you people calling yourselves
The Trogs, why do you do that, that you actually perform
mock marriages and stay overnight together in groups
of *mixed sexes* in these caves and that you have a high
degree of promiscuity due to your mock divorces the following day
could I just ask you, as a member of the Trogs do you
participate in those alleged activities. *I see.* In other words
you consider all those reports false in the sense that your
main activity is just straight fucking, that's very interesting
here this afternoon for those of our fans who are sadistic
voyeurs and I understand there are quite a number of them.
Some of you straighter fans may have wondered why I felt
I could use the word Fucking over the air, that's due to recent
and timely research into the vocabulary of that late
great competitor General DeBall who invented the word
"fouquin" in referring to the NATO presence in France
and I might add right here I'm sure
the thanks of all fans
whichever side you're rooting for thisafternoon
go out to General De Ball for supplying so many
and so many of the *distinguished* members of
the Underdeveloped squad. And now I see they have
just about carried enough of the underdeveloped players
back onto the field to start play, most of you fans
who are new to the Great Playoff
probably aren't used to seeing it done that way
because in the competition strickly between the richer
countries the players are carried *off* the field having started
off in top shape, but that's just one of the many facets
that makes this World Game different and Unusual

166

Still not much happening as yet,
I do notice however that some of the Developed players
have made *totem poles,* using the goal posts
as props, of some of the more lifeless UD's, a unique
sight and a tribute to the imagination of these fine players
who all seem to be in tremendous form in spite of the *lack*
of opportunity to engage the Underdeveloped World team in
sustained play, which brings up the many questions and letters
I've been asked repeatedly Why does the Developed team bother
well it is just another fine tribute to these boys that they
come out here thisafternoon, give unsparingly of their
time and talent to show they care for this great sport and
I don't think it need be said that all over the free world
every one of you fans both here and watching in your homes
can be proud. The world of sport is one of the few activities
where men and women from both sides of the aluminium curtain
can get together in the spirit of free world competition
to work off their conflicting ideologies and lest it be said
as it was of last year's Olympics that the late night meeting
of some of the contestants is going too far, I don't think
any of you fans would dispute me when I say that the time
is not too far off when "fouquin" to borrow General DeBall's
apt coinage, will be one of the major attractions
wherever sportsmen gather, and when that day comes
Ladies and Gentlemen I predict all the rule-books
will go out the window, that's a *close contact* sport
                                        if there ever was one
and one that promises to settle once and for all certain
racial myths which have inevitably grown up over the years here
thisafternoon and one which if it becomes as popular as
non-contact sports could revolutionize human relations everwhere
and as some of you fans may have seen the poll in last weeks
        Newsweek
9 out of 10, that's over half, housewives
were definitely for "fouquin" or fucking, with the underdeveloped
        world.
Unfortunately at this point it is impossible to tell what

the attitude of the yellow UD world is, but from all indications
the population reports from that area indicate "fouquin"
has long been in natural existence.
And now I'll just turn
herethisafternoon to my personal guest Harry Kamikaze who most of
you fans know
as Harry Carry, a former citizen of the Kalmuck Autonomous
Soviet Socialist Republic which was abolished in 1945, at which time
I believe you emigrated and finally settled in St.Louis, is that
right, Harry
Yes. That right Stern Bill. I come St.Louis 1954 tho.
That's tremendously interesting Harry. That means you arrived
in StLouis in 1954 doesn't it, 7 years after 1945, inotherwords
more than half the period of the contest between
the United States and what was then a very small world team, I
shld just remind our fans Harry, that Africa for instance
was one country under the tutelage I believe of Union Miniere,
that very memorable and competitive cartel in what a lot of you
fans nostalgically recall as Darkest africa and which
produced great old performers such as Conrad, and that dual,
taciturn but highly dangerous man on a good day, *Stanley Livingstone*
and of course that very obscure and shifty player Patrice Lamumba
in modern times, but only the very youngest of our fans would
remember his few troubled seasons with the All-Congo
team, one of those promising UD teams which never got off
the ground
their players, as I recall could never get enough food to enable
them to stand up, one of the first pre-requisites to international
competition. And now Harry, could I just briefly ask you
How did your famous association
with Dizzy Bean start
Well, Mr Bill Lot's fans they think
Dizz he from Mississippi or someplace like that but he Japonese
convert like me, during war he enlist on Japonese side, he hero
of one most famous exploit on Japan mainland, very little known
is exploit in which secret regiment negro soldier land miserable
night 1944 plan is to get lost incognito as you so properly say
among mass of Japonese people. They have special assignment being

168

to infiltrate but inaddition initiate velly first international
"fouquin" engagement with result they so satisfyed with enthusiasm
of competition they stay as Japonese having plastic surgery to
shorten legs and epidermous operation to change color from black
to pale yellow, most interesting.

But Harry, just for the information
of our fans, are you suggesting that Dizzy Bean was at that time
a *negro*?

No please, Dizzy Bean in reality originally died-in-wool
whiteman but on hearing of immanent invasion he quick change color
so as participate in first instance what General DeBalls have called
"fouquin."

But this is tremendous, if not incredible, Harry Kamikaze,
are you suggesting the rest of the colored men in the regiment
did not know of this deception.

Yes please, they knew, because Dizzy Bean velly obvious
white man, equipped with forked tongue plus fat head, one must
not forget he famous with ability throw baseball, colored regiment
think Mr. Bean come in as americans say handy, thus, night of landing
only known instance White-Black cooperation occur as Black regiment
hand Dizzy Bean many baseball thus, successful completion of
all but unheardof invasion

That's extremely fascinating Harry and could you just
tell the fans how Dizzy made his *fantastic* way back to St. Louis.

Gladly please. Black regiment know there no use
for Dizzy Bean after honorable invasion so they contrive
situation whereby Dizz be pushed in hot liquid which remove
all vestige of black race, thus, exposed, in all true physical
dimension japonese women put in bottle with message deliver St.Louis
being only american town known in village, subsequently Dizzy Bean
arrive honorable city C.O.D. from San Francisco.

That's one of the great great wrap-up stories
Harry Kamikaze and I'm sure thisafternoonhere the fans

are all wanting to know how *you* got to St.Louis. In other words
how do you explain the period between the ending of the war
with that great great weapon dropped on I've forgotten the name
of the particular Japanese town but it was one of the big events
that year and now.

very willingly, please. At time Dizzy Bean in bottle
slowly making way San Francisco I, now Harry Carry, am
in Kalmuck Autonomous Soviet Socialist Republic still tranquil
person. I next go alaska disguised as esquimo who all look alike
as I do. There, I receive message written illiterate southern
dialect I think japonese translation of russian appeal for Kamikaze
pilot to carry on war single handed after soon to be end
for japonese team. I very out of touch among esquimo. In reality
message sent by Dizzy Bean in other bottle on way to San Francisco
say merely HELP. In confusion I enlist in japonese air corps as
special post war suicide diver. Years later I discover much to
honorable surprise Korean war seperate engagement I participate
in ignorance. Then make way St. Louis.

That was a fabulous account Harry
of your many sporting adventures
and all the fans were thrilled I'm sure
to have that account from you yourself.
and now fans this second quarter
is almost over and still there doesn't seem to be
any noteworthy action and very little prospect
herethisafternoon at least in this current period
so I'll just take this opportunity before the half
to explain what seems to be one of the more burning
questions a lot of you sportsfans have out there
from the letters and complaints, enqueries of all
sorts we've received. Namely, what happens to the *used*
underdeveloped players. I know some people have heard
the carcasses of UD players are used in Dr. Ross Dog and Cat food
and that *was* true in the early days of the series
but as there *were* so many complaints from Animal Lovers
especially in the Developed countries Dr.Ross hasnot

used that source as a major ingredient for the past few seasons.
Dog and Cat lovers all over the free world
questioned the hygiene of such practice
and it was found by independent research organizations
that the nutritional value of underdeveloped people
was generally low and not consistently high enough
to support the life of a dog, however, thanks
to a very forward looking Rhodesian
housewife named Mrs. Smith who experimented for *years*
a way has been found to save at least a part of the body.
Mrs. Smith, purely by accident one day found a book
which had fallen off a shelf onto the body of a dead negro
in her garage in Salisbury. Upon pulling the book
away some of the skin stuck, and in this way this simple
otherwise unsophisticated housewife *re*discovered
one of the lost sporting uses for skin and now
conducts one of the few flourishing businesses
in that country threatened by antisport factions. I might
just add for the benefit of those of you listeners
who want to conduct your own experiments that Mrs Smith
found thru later experience that those skins of black nationals
who die under conditions of terrific pain
are the most interesting, colorwise and texturewise.
It isn't known as yet why this is so but apparently it
is true of all underdeveloped skins, recent experiments
in Southeast Asia have shown results to be the same.

And now I believe there are
only a few seconds left in the second quarter which didn't *quite*
get off the ground and I think will end having had no action at all
but I hope everybody will stand by for the great *half-time*
festivities coming up in less than two minutes.

THE HALFTIME SCRIPT

This is *Stern Bill* back in the box overlooking
the new "Hope of the Freeworld" Yanqui-go-home stadium
and thanking sportsfans the world over for their

great patience herethisafternoon in one of the best
and most inventive if actionless playoffs in recent years.
One of the problems *of* the World Playoff incidentally
is the fact that as the Underdeveloped Nations
become more developed, there is going to be
bound to be this problem of what to do during the
actual game, how to keep the interest and attention
of the many fans the world over who look forward all year
to this great event. It has been suggested and not without
some validity in the view of lots of fans
that play be dispensed with altogether and the
what you might call *ceremonial function*, the burning
smashing, crushing, and the more sophisticated outlets
such as underdeveloped eyeball removal with powerful plastic
sucking straws introduced last year by the cocacola bottling company
could become the main feature of the Playoffs
but there are lots of traditional fans who would hate
to see that kind of change in the rules
they argue that the game would degenerate rapidly
into simple entertainment. John Malcom Fuggeridge, for example
is one of the fans who feels strongly that the game
should not be changed and very shortly we'll interview him
and his curiously dressed companion, but before we get to
our great lineup of Halftime guests, let's go back down
to the field for a view of the Halftime performances from both
sides in this contest heretoday.
                           It goes without saying
that buffs and fans everywhere have waited for *at least* this stellar
excitement. For many years now the Halftime ceremonies have been
spectacular *in that* they dramatically play *up* the differences
the many predictable and sometimes unpredictable differences
between these so completely *different* and yet in *so many ways*
strangely alike teams except for their color and all that
goes *with* that
               This year as last
the Haves are moving onto the field with what they *have*
and the Havenots are standing aside with their magnificent,
primordial even, bodies, nude mostly except here and there
in the motley crowd there is a visitor who has somehow

172

in God Knows What fashion managed to dress in what can only
be described
                as impetuous, no holds barred, *splashy* even,
color, fans have only to look as the camera now catches
the tahitian contingent, these handsome subjects of Gen. DeBalls
who you will remember we mentioned earlier in the game as
having contributed so much to world understanding
if only as a start, with his new close-contact conception
"fouquin," a concept both worlds understand and respond to
almost involuntarily *if only* the immense problems
can be solved which most simply put, for the understanding
of all you simple straight fans out there, is how
to set the game up so as not to make the lights *darker*
or the darks *lighter.* Altho there has been one suggestion
for that *specific* problem, it's what might come to be called
"the litmus race test" where a bacteria soaked paper
can actually be placed on the skin which will show
beyond a shade of doubt that any darkening, this is
for the developed, traditionally Have peoples, comes from
the ordinary Suntan Pill, or in the case of most
Ordinary Fans, just what we might call *plain exposure*
to sun, the bacteriological paper will work likewise
to show color to be inherited, permanent, that is
year-round . . . out of consideration to Underdeveloped sensibilities.

                So onto the field herethisafternoon
come the dazzling sportcars of the Haves decorated
as usual with those endlessly smiling infinitely *young*
girls renown throughout the Developed World wearing
as for the past several years Nothing At All only a pale
yellow *Rose of Texas* in their Amplenavels, otherwise
ruddy, pink and *cheerful selfconfidence* as our fans have
naturally come to expect from those spotlessly chosen
superbly legged contestants, one disturbing note herethisafternoon
some dark clouds were seen in the West. And now here are those
floats depicting the history of the Haves a mixture of our
rich past, all the major slaveholding states are represented,
Greece Rome and then the subsequent minor nations of

173

western Europe France Germany Spain England
The Scandinavian Countries, *Russia* somewhat unused to this
procedure has a rather boring float, machines for the most part
and the *moon* which you spectators plus of course *everyone*
else have been waiting for since the announcement last January
that it has been shrunk and towed back especially for these
great international games. The question remains in the minds
of many viewers just how will it be returned to its proper
place in the sky, and to get to the answer to that *important*
question we have arranged an interview with the Russian
Minister of Transportation Ivan Transferinsky who will
join us following John Malcom Fuggeridge and his
                              as I said before Curiously Dressed
Companion.
      And before we join our roving mike and *John Malcom*
a brief commentary on the Havenot floats which are *just now*
after that gloriously long line of lasciviously designed
machinery and womanhood from the developed *Have* side has passed,
coming onto the field now is all the Havenots can muster
an amazing mixture of colorful misunderstanding and *interesting*
naiveté for which these people are noted, I'm sure most fans
as usual find this part of halftime ceremony familiar—
the same as in previous years the floats are merely propaganda—
a Boring pre-occupation with food and the usual exhortations
to *Grow* More, or else as in the case with Basutolands float
boring and nearly pornographic native dances
altho I *will say* most of the *Zulu* women on these floats
look anything *But* Underdeveloped herethisafternoon with
the sun still shining down but more and blacker clouds now
gathering on all the horizons. Some aspects of the Underdeveloped
floats have been traditionally incomprehensible to Western
Developed understanding, one-*half* of the *Tanzania* float
is taken up with a display of *shrunken* heads cleverly contrived
to look as tho they had been White originally, the curious
fact being of course herethisafternoon that those peoples
are not known to be headhunters traditionally,
as the books tell us.
And last but not least a prominent place is given on the Havenot

floats to *witchdoctors* and all the quaint paraphernalia
that goes with former practices, great black pots of blood
labeled White blood stirred constantly by grinning blackmen
with those colorful traditional bones in their noses, all the fun
you fans have come to anticipate and expect from the final playoff
of the World Cupleague Serious. Various tribes, according
to where they reside have labeled the blood specifically to point
toward definite Have countries, for example the Southwestafrican
float's pot is labeled *Boer Blood,* Angola's contingent
has their pot marked *Blood Portuguese* and so on, all the ribaldry
of free exchange you fans have come to expect from the Series.
The only float in *bad taste* I've noticed here this afternoon
is the one from Mississippi USA which depicts a black man, a tremendous,
powerfully built black man, the only word for it is *raping*
judging from their relative positions and the action
a White Woman whom they've taken the added precaution of labeling
White, lest any of you fans out there fail to get the point
and as if this weren't enough it looks from here
like they've towed the woman's pale blue sportscar behind the float
simply to reinforce the point that she is indeed
part of the Developed, really Developed World Here,
                         this now darkening afternoon

         The signal from our roving mike has come thru
from our interviews altho the camera will occasionally
as the action merits flash back to the field.

         And now to our roving mike and John Fuggeridge
who, for many of you fans is the arbiter of what *is* happening
in the I can only say Modern World thisafternoon, *What*
Mr. Fuggeridge is your impression of this great contest
and *Who,* because I know all the fans are *dying* to know,
is your curiously dressed companion, please, you must talk
Louder and plainer Mr. Fuggeridge, there is so much Plastique
going off around the pressbox we can transmit you Only
with the greatest difficulty
                    You say *you think the event is Corny!*
What do you mean by that, here, this great afternoon, here

175

at the World Final, the Playoff between the Haves, those fabulously
resourceful, you take the low road and I'll get high, those
competitors par excellence, *against* that part of the world
which, to say the least, has traditionally Lost.

I thot you said

What! *Cruelty?* I think the connection is being interfered with
at least on this end my spotter with binoculars says a Havenot
is chewing on our *roving mike wire,* yes thankyou Mr. Fuggeridge
our camera shows your curiously dressed assistant, I mean companion
has just given that unidentified blackman a sandwich whereby
cleverly diverting his attention, just one of the many contingencies
Fans, which arise unpredictably at such an event as this thisafternoon.
Now to continue as long as communication lasts under these
unusual, perhaps even unpredictable conditions this is *Stern Bill*
from the new, even sweeping, Yanqui-go-home stadium in downtown
Neutral, Nowhere, bringing you the Payoff, pardon me Playoff
between the usual contenders, Sorry about that interruption John
but to get back to your opinion of this afternoon's event
what is your estimation of the Quality this year

My God, Stern Bill, have you actually been watching
this wretched debacle?

Well of course John Malcom, as you say, this is the *Event*
more than half the world has been waiting for and while we're *on*
that subject John Malcom Fuggeridge just let me ask you
who indeed is your mystery companion herethisafternoon, your,
as I said earlier, *curiously dressed* companion

Stern Bill I didn't say that, but anyway, *that's*
not my companion, that's Trustworthy Kaput, the famous,
as you would say, *Fabulous,* southern degenerate and author
of *A Lukewarm Dud,* actually I wouldn't call it a book
it's far greater, far *deeper,* far more gripping
than any book could be, which is set, my GOD Stern Bill
I'm talking like you, anyway, it's set in the sleepy, average
town of Monkey Balls Kansas, and is the story of ordinary people
in other words typically *Have,* midwestern people

176

who find themselves one evening in the clutches of ordinary killers,
and Trustworthy here, who as you may have read is the routine friend,
when he isn't traipsing off to Monkey Balls, of world leaders
all of whom are so obvious that to *not* mention them
is to mention them, do you *comprehend* such a paradox Stern Bill,
and furthermore my companion is *not* curiously dressed *at this,*
as you would say, if I can in all good natured fun quote you,
Actionpact, Superfun World playoff.

I never said that John Malcom, words like Actionpact
and Superfun I *never* use, all the fans recognize those words as
part of the cynical conspiracy which has as its *ultimate aim*
to undermine the very sense of high sportsmanship this *great*
game rests on.

You must be joking, Stern Bill.

Of course, John Malcom Fuggeridge, that kind of banter
is just a small, though *important* small part of the great
sport spirit, but you say you are *not* curiously dressed and yet
I notice you and your companion Trustworthy Kaput are dressed
as Batman and Robin. Don't you think that's a little out of date
or are you *intentionally* out of date in order to be *in* date
in order, in other words, to *enhance* your already great reputation
herethisafternoon at this great, perhaps one of the *greatest*
playoffs we have yet witnessed.

I won't answer that Stern, I mean you're just contemptible
and furthermore Trustworthy has binoculars too and I warn you
has noticed that you have been smoking constantly, probably one
of the reasons you repeat yourself so unnecessarily.

That's very interesting J.M., as you must know earlier
we interviewed that old standby Harold "Harry" Carry who gave
our listeners and viewers some incisive insights into todays
play I wonder if Trustworthy Kaput wld be willing to say a few words.

Hello Thtern Bill, I think you're worth than a murderer

177

letting all those Underdeveloped people thtarve and languish
on the playingfields of Eton and not even caring as you *mothcertainly*
don't, you are *too* cold and one day the forces of justice
will catch up with you and then you won't be able to thay *anything*
especially about such people as this, whom I have with *my own eyes*
seen you be most callous about, wee fwippant about their lack
of clothes and the condition they're in of malnourishment but *besides*
that Thtern Bill, youre just a cheap, popular commentatior, *you*
never, or probably *almost* never, get down into the real contact
such people as these require, you have no idea at all what
you are watching and besides you're just smug. A quick tongue
can drop off—Love it or Leave it, Thtern Bill.

That's a great insight herethisafternoon Mr. Kaput
and I'm sure all you fans appreciate the time
these two fantastically important men so willingly Gave
to give you their Great Impressions

It prompts me to say that I hope all you fans out there will *buy*
Trustworthy Kaput's trailmaking opus *A Lukewarm Dud* because
inspite of what Ken Tynan, one of our 1st quarter guests says
there is no other such book that deals with the peculiar problems
of Monkey Balls Kansas in quite so Poignant a way and now
it looks like the finale to the great Halftime celebration
is entering its final phase with the colorful and colored
marching bands entering the field and I believe we have time
to pick up our roving mike again all you fans who have to go
to the toilet whether following this great game from the stands
or in the privacy of your own home stand by for the interview
of the Half. Our man in the stands has been granted permission
to interview Elizabeth Taylor's four dogs currently residing
on a yacht moored in the Thames and attending the great spectacle
herethisafternoon by special permission of a few fairminded and
sportsminded labor M.P.s . . .

THESIS

             Only the Illegitimate are beautiful
             and only the Good
       proliferate only the Illegitimate
       Oh Aklavik only you are beautiful
     Ah Aklavik your main street is dead
       only the blemished are beautiful only
         the deserted have life made
           of whole, unsurpassable night
            only Aklavik is life inside life inside
itself.
               They have gone who walk stiltedly
      on the legs of life. All life is
     in the northern hemisphere turning around
the radicals of gross pain and great joy
       the poles of pure life move
             into the circle of
           our north, oh Aklavik only
             the outcast and ab
     andoned to the night are faultless
      only the faultless have fallen only
       the fallen are the pure Children of the Sun
only they move West, only they are expected,
         in the virgin heat
         by those who wait intensely
     for the creatures from the East, only
     Aklavik, our Aklavik, is North
       and lovely, always abandoned
     always dark, whose warp is light.
     Simple fear compels Inuvik, her liquor store
        lifts the darkness
           by the rotation of a false summer.
       The Children of the Sun never go
     to Inuvik, on bloody feet, half starved,

or suffering the absolute intrusion
of any food oh Aklavik they vomit
on your remote and insupportably obscure streets
which run antiseptically into the wilderness
and if blackflies inhabit with the insistence
of castenets the delta of Inuvik in you Aklavik
around you Aklavik they form a core
and critical shell of inflexible lust, only
in the permafrost
is the new home of the Children
of the Sun in whose nakedness
is the desire not desire
in whose beauty is the flame of red
permafrost a thousand feet deep in whose
frail buildings
the shudder of total winter in whose
misshapened sun the Children bathe

THE FIRST NOTE (FROM LONDON

As we go
through Sussex, hills are round
bellies are the downs
pregnantly lovely
the rounds of them, no towns
the train passes
shaking along the groove
of the countryside.
Travel to Newcastle is
west of the moors or
east of the western moors, between it all
one goes, and everything is aye! and bonnie

Cold then, the note is, Katmandu
the outward point.
How far the people see
in a naturally cold place

pots of tea
and a collection of fires.

So lovely she is England
with her swollen bellies
                        all the way
to the stone cardboard of Brighton
    pale this winter,
        a paper jewel
            whose regent strolled

        We got into one of those old coaches
        which has no access
forward or back but is self contained
and it was strained being so enclosed and locked off
by the speed of passage, alone
                            and even though
she was my wife we flirted
almost, we were almost in our confusion shy
scarcely believing our situation so sealed off.

We considered of course making it then and there
while moving

        but settled for a quiet kiss when halfway through it
abruptly and to our amazement
we found ourselves in some small station smiling
into the equally smiling face
of a railway man idling
on that minor and unremembered platform, nonetheless
we were sober and chaste
and slightly disappointed
from thence to Croydon

ENGLAND, ITS LATITUDE AND SOME OF ITS CONDITIONS,
THE SERIOUSNESS OF GHOSTS

More north than
        most casual laborers know.
So cold.
From the center of
        the earth
the line comes up to
                pierce
        any man
can't understand
        what gravity is
that he has an
        ordered and
endlessly transferrable
        \   place
So cold
        you wake up
                mumble some complaint
        to yourself.
Black comes into the senses
more than green. One day
there came on Lexden Road
        a long, high hearse
with a sloping back like a
        medium hill.
        a man in funereal garments
rode shotgun
                his face under the black
                top hat
        a grinning
        memento mori

        as if it were all happening
        long ago and inside a woodcut
        depicting Elizabeth's times.
Two attendants sit soberly

in the back with the body.
The Rooks raise an ominous sign
over the church and then resettle
around their bold nests high in the trees.

The corpse seems to possess no life
and the undertakers try to match
the imagined state of the dead man.
the funeral limousine moves very slowly
the man in top hat trains his eye

on the line
of the white road ahead, the procession, Moses,
moves slowly ahead, all your hard laws
have come to a bad end. We are so goddamn weary.
          there are flowers on top and inside
the hearse, red white and pink flowers
          the sign of the dead. The "creations"
with a special scent, never
          the wild wood flowers
          with a delicate almost absent scent
          the flowers of heavy demand
the fake rich odor we associate with
                              the end
                    the fake solemnity
               of the bell
          the rank proper smell
     of death
          ah when did we become so anxious
     in the proof
     of our relief
     that the dead
     be gone
     when we have always
     and without the final tremor
been so glad to have
          our noses
          broke

                    for the glamour of
                        our faces
when did we dare begin the association of flowers
with our routine deaths.

Ghosts complete our present.
We would rush to Hadrian's wall
where *Life* photographers
a symbiosis for to seek
of America and Rome
arrived breathless
like any other commodity-killer
EXPECTATION
to find the motherfucker covered
a "natural" occurrence of winter
with *snow*.
Blackout.
(miserable, uncooperative
no matter
another day—(if they
remember—the expense account
affords such forgetfulness
that an organized people
at least built a wall
that respect to the barbarian
technology was not
so neat it made them
foam blankets, a wall!
each stupid stone laid
is what they made, latin inscription
on posts
                Note: if the americans built a wall
                         in Vee-et (past tense of ate)
                         NAM, they would at least leave
                         something behind as *made*—the
                         way stations could even have texan
                         inscriptions which will retain
                         their exoticism for 2000 years

who now
knows the way by stone,
who has the letters of guidance
the speech is
still understood. Not
for Picts. No message for Picts
but what the 5th legion
can manage with swords
and the pointed mass
of that arrangement—
            War is fair enough.
            you *shall* be killed if
you are alive. Violence
is the only act
that makes life
a message
for anyone
who would build towers
in Texas
and ascribe *causes*
to *condition*: EXmarine
Eagle Scout
crew cut
underarm deodorant.
            T-shirt.
It's a long way from home
for an italian.

A THEORY OF TRUTH
THE NORTH ATLANTIC TURBINE

> *"The world is round. Only one-third of*
> *its people are asleep at any given moment.*
> *The other two-thirds are awake and probably*
> *stirring up mischief somewhere."*

—Secretary Rusk
(*Time,* Atlantic edition,
Feb. 4, 1966)

not *includes* west africa
goes to west africa
rum slaves and crude molasses
Wilberforce a standard trick
of conscience, what i.e.,
can be *thought* of man
as he ventures
part of Bristol is still rich.

       it starts of course
with the *finished* product
nothing starts with the 1st.
Nothing. The end
is first. Always.
There is no beginning
unless the end
has been reached. First.
The second is the middled
and that may be people
or some other material.
Molasses or molasses skinned persons.
the turbine is only movement.
the current of the atlantic
swirl,

     This is no rose
this is the turbine. Continents
break before it

they pull apart to allow
the pass—it takes only
a few million years
to produce any given Cleveland
Violence is the last chipping
away
        the ice falls
the bulk bobs up
it isn't race or nation governs
movement

        Movement
occurs at the split
displacement is a sign
We are told the signs
are men. Men rot.
Trade revolved and revolves
it remains the turbine
the atlantic turgidity
defines still our small era
that's the exploitation people
mean
when they say they
hear a symphony.

    The fact is there is no art
    no vision in the West there is no
definition cannot be made the "reason"
for unalterable and predictable action.
You could see
how it operated in antediluvian Florence
men there must have thought they
"made" something more than protective walls
not against water, against men—
(The central difference between Medieval
and Renaissance is simply expanded commercial enterprise,
isn't that the "spirit of the age"?
Ghiberti's doors are the doors

to the biggest bank, and bank doors
may be "the gate to paradise." The Baptistry
is clearly a bank (those doors
would fit the Chase Manhattan as well)
tourists have never mistaken that—
the iron grating was put up
to protect the gold being rubbed off
by their inquisitive fingers.

The French now, after Vietnam, are
"moral" but the american astronauts
failed to see the French signal from the Sahara
a current U.S. memorial stamp
celebrates the Polish millennium.
          "Trade has increased is what that means.

                    "I am the creature
from the north atlantic. I will speak
now of the circulation of my discontent
and of that dull unhappiness which,
on the occasions of their excitement,
all creatures describe. Total war
has been uninstructive,
                    a Krupp
will arise from the classic flame, civil
war tears the heart and trade flourishes
                    doubly.

"The turbine moves clockwise
on the northern surface.

          "As long as its base
stays—solutions outside that bind
can come from Plato and Walter Brennan
to no effect.
                    "The first 'modern' state
                    (the gold power to inflate specie)
                    was Spain who saves herself

by remaining socially Medieval
Bolivia y Venesuela son
tambien
naciones
no son continentes

"Can't you see
my love the simplicity is
to reverse the stream at first—
to kill it
and then to move Switzerland back into the back yard
if that be
our governing body. Like one of those cute
painted, plaster dwarfs.

"We need *all* the money. The money
has to be total and it has to be totally deflated
It must be worth everything. One man
must have *all* of it. *All* men
must have *all* of it. Every man
must, and will or he will kill,
have *all* the money.

"Listen, we have had to put up with used shit
from the beginning. I was presented
with a 'dull idea' *before*
I was given a nipple. That 'idea'
was 'life on earth' which
wrapped in all that could be easily
and hurriedly grabbed was supposed
to appeal to me. It didn't. Was
an automobile supposed to be
my Royal car to heaven? or
some lousy and antique chariot?
not so fanciful that. Piggott
mentions a modern case of wagon-burial
at Garsington, within sight of Oxford.

189

Into the caravan of the lately deceased 'mother'
of a clan of 400 were placed her possessions,
including the harness worn by the horses.
It was then burnt, the two horses,
were killed as well as her three servants
one of the relations saying that
'the ritual must be observed.' Finally
the pots and pans were smashed
and with the parts surviving
the fire, were buried in a pit.
Quite true, my dear. *The Times,* 13 Jan. 1953.
No. Somebody is going to put his
grubby fingers right through it
going to take the property of old brigadiers
and burn it. The property of middle aged
and graduate dentists. Doctors
and lawyers are going to be told to
manifestly bugger themselves as a *gratuity.*
It will be the one *experience* of their lives
and the children of the 'underdeveloped'
are going to make playground equipment
of all those ornate chairs.

Idylls of knaves. Better Homes and Gardens!
Of course, that's not true, those old hogs
will keep on a wallowin forever

"But forget them! They can piss oatmeal.
I was saying . . .
The hours burn now as if they were individual candles.
That's just too bad but only 'real' estate
and a few motor vehicles—but think
of blowing the foundation away from
those buildings like 'Empire,' 'state.'
Oh yea and putting dynamite in the bungs
of elephants whole zoos BANG!
go up via their holes which are
'natural' depositories

while the smiling well fed 'children'
of those 'people' who think up
things to do after sunday dinner watch.
For instance the 'Berkeley professor'
who said he was 'pleased' when a 'student'
offered him pot, it meant they
trusted him, is imbued
with the delight of the urbanite
he also loves a parade
in the same sense he enjoys
anthropological folk singers
and is a fan of Baseball fans
you register that?
                    As if they
'were made for it' say
ever think of a zoo like that
just a collection of holes
you could just *drop* it of course
in a kangaroo's pouch. (Sorry
Australia, you fink. Too Bad no
interesting animals come from S. Africa.

                    "The zoo is animal property.
Like women. They don't make war.
They are not in 'the wrong village,'
as they say of certain situations in Vietnam.
Our atlantic turbine turns clockwise.
it is that simple minded.

"Here luv, this is a list of property to be blown apart
along the North Atlantic perimeter—
last things first as usual:
1. financial consortia or power money then
          (in that destructive petty TRADE
          the main circulatory energy
          of the turbine, will go as a
          secondary effect—specific persons, the corner grocer,
                              as they say.

191

"2. The functionaries of the fiscal apparatus
'computers' and the entire secretariatus
all construction equipment
such as cranes, 'caterpillars'
the entire class of 'earth movers,'
anything electric, anything metal
anything with a lever or button
anything painted yellow not red,† anything
which makes even a remotely
internal combustion.
    in short: anyone holding
    more than $15, £5, 8750 lire
    500 drachmae etc.
    This will rid the world
    in one stroke
    of the 'majority,' its most perniciously useful people.

† "Red is a capital color as a matter of fact
flags and new machines are mostly red
red persons are rarely communist
—I remember Red Gillens, the terror
of my home town in the late forties
was so articulate he became a delinquent
while in school, and later on in life
a small time capitalist. On the other hand
there is Lee Harwood the English poet comma
a red person comma who is so delicate
he can discover the Western Hemisphere
now as of year 1491.

"3. All natural resources
from which the foregoing
might be built.†

† "note: 'Natural resources have been
the first way men
have been put down:
to exploit the immediate surroundings

192

and then themselves at large, and if
resources have been absent
the unlucky have had to settle
for a moral lesson: *buy or die.*
Since the original design of the earth
left no area lacking in *some*
resource deprivation has always
meant 'lack of machinery.'
Natural resources generate the unnatural—
      (not the 'super' natural,
           which is creative)
      is a basic paradox

"4.   Finally, the earth as primary object
     must be destroyed. This is a difficult
     sense. The #4 is a pointless number.
     (it is the transition number
     (Death, the 3rd and the 1st.   [the 2nd. he of one series
     which is the Four.)   & the Yod of the next.]
     The earth has been destroyed. Only a
     few people know that. The rest usually
     think of it as a subject of some threat;
     atomic, nuclear, erosional
     etc. What must be destroyed is
     the present circus of the earth and
     the place to start is the North
     Atlantic turbulence
           English pound
             swiss
               banker
                 mini
                   skirt
                     the american law
                      of the nickel
                      cigar,
                    or
                       How to Make
                        Trees

                              Out of
                              Sawdust,
                                 w/howdy-do
                                 you all
or, as if to greet you w/   I'm from alabama
a vocabularial gesture of the middle finger   on every
known in some regions as 'the bird'   leaf
may I suggest we all change our present names
to J.P. Getty: we all then emigrate from Minnesota
w/a million skins in our jeans, something to begin with.
and while we seem in our adventures to be merely
screwing the farmers' daughters we are
in 'reality' skimming the cream from the top
of her pail. 'Naturally' we 'eventually' tire
of the Vulgarity of the United Statesety and
Settle In London, until, again with a vocabularial
gesture, we 'admit' that, altho the Bunnies' thighs
are hot and Hugh Hefner thinks our gonads
are composed of solid philosophy, the fact is,
it is just too damn cold and our asses are freezing
in an 18th century manner. Dispirited at last,
and for good cause since our guests are more interested
in our money than in our philosophy, we install a pay phone
in the unheated Great Hall to stop their nicking
transatlantic conversations, and declare the immensely rich
(a term in our 'realism' we have come to use w/out embarrassment)
to be the most lonely of all peoples, whereupon
we empty the coins from the phone, grab a bunny by the tit
and split for Rome, find a largish pad on a hill
what won't flood, hang up 'our' paintings, throw
a party (Hello Dolly, Howdy do Tex, Barbara Madbutt there,
glad you all could come) and settle 'down.'

        "Big *system*! China-and-the-East
        is simply an amateur West
        in crude contradiction.
        Any mass gadget can prolong,
        as it adds to, world pain.

194

The equipment of the commodity-motivated killer is the
thing under your nose. Whitman carried
into the administration tower of the U. of Takes-us
        underarm spray deodorant. I
date the urgency as before reversions ie.,
*auto*mobiles reach China."

        End-O-China

OXFORD

PART I: FORNICATION

From Paddington
along one of the radials of London

    Which are the Oxford Types
    in the coach, the girl
    with the swell legs
"Oxford has some of the richest
    and most beautiful women
        in the world"
    The sunday supplement said.
The one from Argentina,
the one from Portugal, a couple of straight
american girls too clean to be real
rich unquestionably.
                A Swedish girl, all weird countries
        and variously do their cunts shine
        with radiant national deposits, a
        kind of enlightenment
                        (if you will)

195

Enlightened self interest, those care packages
are kept at home until full grown
then sent abroad
                    wrapt in fur

We are witness to all it is possible
with such instruments
                    as nations
                    and mellifluous boxes
          to suck up
          the part of the world they may in any given period
     have wanted
and which they do want
          alias The Good Life, this is
          their most rigid virtue
          and not importantly Education.

                    They perpetuate their own kind
in that way
with old visions of Congolese uranium in the air
while the stolidly engaged back home cry out
to Bolivar
thinking that is where they are
                    The music of that desire
is a richly orchestrated tapestry
of instruction for their daughters, here
teach them to ruin you, answer their questions.
Or because mass production allows
a visual proximity and burns out the memory in men
of the past two centuries, tie your shoelaces
and wear a protective grin.

     But on the vistas of the hot plain back home
the quivering form is murder
of course, the rest of the imperialism
implied by their shapely legs
is of not much consequence. Naval stores, no.
And copra or hemp, no. Argentina just turns
over when asked, like any other whore. Just murder:

the only ecstasy opposite the equal sign
of these recent centuries.
                              The woman opposite me
by no other act than Murder
is permitted existence. Nothing less
will shape and spread
those legs. And it is only one of
those known habits like thinking gravity is real
because the apple fell, that the apple was rotten
or that a relentless wind blew
or in a different tense how the rich screw
is equally uninteresting.

        She got off the train in Reading
pronounced *Red*ing. I yawned a little
riding through Reading.
Such a beautiful woman of caution.

It isn't the plateaus which intrigue me
with their sexual halftones, the moonlight/
on the warped boards of men's lives is all
it is, the plantations of old habits, the smoke
of freedom curls up from every shack
in the region, if you can see it it's time
to move on, open up more country, keep busy
or go mad or how about that inturned coldness
of the English man
                    breaking to the surface
                    at the slightest turn
                    a kind of warmth sometimes
                    and the women with their uncontrollable
                    voices, deadly *are* their gestures, their
                    mannish self assurance and brittle their laughter

        The bull, mounted
we both saw at the same time
out the window in the rolling green fields
which sweep off the low lying Chilterns,
what did she think? that I had *willed* it

as a suggestion to her,
          I didn't even know her. But because Mars
rules me and she watched us both briefly
the red bull in the field in the rushing window
was up in his position, went into the female creature
below him, one of fifty,
the others possessed also by the earth
immensely soft muzzles to the grass
did she think *I* was *thinking*
in that crowded compartment
immersed in the smell of people
that by looking, coupled to me by triangulation
we shared an Act—I had by implication mounted her?
It couldn't have been *embarrassment,* we were on a train
the cows were in the field. That by *looking*
we shared an act?

The contrary of what we all say is heartbreak (when
no one mistakes caution. Be done.
It is not the end that matters
In the begin-ning
          there was Everybody
          they smiled
          as they said goodbye.

PART II: IN TOWN

The sands of the Cotswolds
     line the streets, the stone portals
   a light of light brown brilliance
when the suns of May
     cast a black swatch
by Radcliffe Camera
                    solitary as
               any Baptistry encrusted
          or a product
     of the sea.
     However the streams of thin

198

elegance come down past the town
it is the linear strip
of the beautiful Jurassic lias
running from Flixborough in Lincolnshire
hanging from there
this liana falls, lier
as the most springing joint
of England
to Bristol

PART III: COMFORTED BY LIMESTONE

The blocks
which are the buildings and walls
All Souls
come from lower Oolite
the upper Oolite
the portland beds
and Corallian
are for burning lime, placed
between the two, fallen from
the north Oxford is cut off from
the Chilterns
the massive chalk which ends
its arc
in a thin lip eastward from
King's Lynn and upon
an edge
Cambridge sits.
snagged on the Cretaceous bank
as the land flows
towards the Wash
and the Lynn Deeps

I come to Oxford
not with the illiteracy with which
I could be
          accused, but with eyes
cold most of all to the blandishments
I was most ready
at first
to assume were appropriate.

    I am a stranger on this continent
and more a stranger on this detached
                         fragment of it.
     The Aubrey holes sunk into this land
seem, by their art,
          to me, as throbbing
      in their intimacy
          as the lunar intimacies
          they signify, or the dropped H
          and glottic T
      as suspended in time. To love
               that, and retain an ear for
      the atrocities of my own hemisphere

          more relevant and major for both of us now
England
          is the labor.
What they do in Freeborn County Minnesota is *more* my business.
I grew up with death. I do not   .
need to be reminded of anything
by Europe, least of all do the easy
                    corrections
          of England
               instruct me—
      we share orogeny
               it isn't ignorance
      we have *applied* that,

or what we inherited, perfectly
it was in the invention of our own
ignorances we had
no guiding hand
to dismount the old model

"In a shining cloud of vanity,
dogmatism and political snobbishness
John Adams was inaugurated
president of the united States. Stately Washington,
full of years, honors, errors, courage, honesty,
dullness,
bowed to the world and retired to private life.
Thomas Jefferson,
with his Democratic Societies at his heels,
moved into the position of vice-president.
It was like moving a department store
into a four-room cottage. Alexander Hamilton,
pensively looking on and detesting both Adams
and Jefferson, recalculated possibilities
in the manner of a man
at the races
who has bet on the wrong
horse both ways.
Thomas Pinckney, mystified aspirant,
vanished
into the silences of his library and rose garden"

We are *all* in the sarsen circle.
We are *all* in the *da nang.* Even the Shades
All

of our numbers come up
Russia and china jockey,
it is not race, "La révolte
de Los Angeles
est une révolte contre La Marchandise
contre le monde de la Marchandise

et du travailleur—
consommateur hierar
chiquement
soumis aux mesures
de la Marchandise."
"Les noirs Americains
sont le produit de l'industrie
moderne au meme titre
que l'electronique,
la publicité et le cyclotron."
or, to take it from my country
"In Harlem
it is almost common knowledge
that the Jews etc.,
will go
the next time there's a large
'disturbance,' like they say"

the ugly faces of the news
determine what you shall know
It is that literacy of determination, that
determining sign
"he told me they were discussing Egypt"
(dec. 7 / 1953
England
where rich Freelance sociologists
think Harlow is a more hopeful matriculation
than Cambridge
or Essex
Hastings
in the lower jaw of the alligator, where Harold's
Housecarls rode their horses
to be slaughtered when they dismounted to fight
while crafty Bill's men kept their seats (of power
What did Ike have
to say to Winston?
(Ike is the fat man who remained
relatively skinny

the more senile to the whimpering apparatus
of his "memoirs")
He said, about Russia,
a whore who might change
her clothes
but would appear in the streets,
her traffic unchanged

But churchill was convinced
he could talk to Malenkov
Ike said we ought not
pay any more attention to McCarthy
Winston said Is there no fish? who
ordered the dinner? when after the soup
there was steak. Henri, flown
from Calgary produced whitebait
almost as if . . . all the while
Anthony waited, heir to
oh my god, Suez? Could it be
any more clear
a course was omitted
Bermuda, 1953
the beat generation was born
out of that, and
if they say it was a social movement
finally, it was intellectual
most, it had to be
if the comedy at the top
but perhaps not so level discussions
of the times, the literateness of those times
the most asylumed of this century.
Everybody admits
churchill was a fool.
No one needed to say
Eisenhower was a fool, he carried
his own placard. It said *Kansas*
and *Texas.* Signs.
But
the standard of that time

importantly antecedent to us,
Churchill, was a bedwetting,
stroke-numbed physical imbecile
and rhetoric his last world-tampering,
bad-dinner refuge—he could still
discount the Frogs
                                who were harmless
            and without rockets and gold
                        at that time.
            Men still blame it on McCarthy.
            Literate men!

                        It isn't a matter of cleaning
            one's own house, was never more
            than that chinese free enterprise
Literacy is no longer the same test
it was, or how far can
you raise the skirt
without taking it off
and still call it "social revolution."
If Hunger is a camp flick your blood
shall flow at Oxford (where all those souls
are the most trivial time and motion study types
among you
who imagined themselves as "managers"
but who turn on *after hours* like anyone else))
and its environs, those factory
workers, as Fanon said,
will not be spared, no matter
                        how much
they speak as I heard them, in
                        the Red Lion
                  that rainy night
waiting on the literature society
of how the economics of it
are managed, they all have
import-export minds   not seeing
that the goods

are apt to be demanded straight
from the griddle, no delay
                    at all.
literacy always was bound up with what
men want
        and now that they have been told
    they can *have* what they want,
they want it. They shall soon start
chewing the earth itself, and not in metaphor.
And poets, no matter what their language
or the size their thorax have
all along chewed *with* them / men
will one day not tolerate
Bedwetting leaders, unless that pee
can be explained as more than private transfer
and not the "balance"
of payments or those colorful but incompetent
shop assistants or the incredibly misplaced
dissidence of the woolworth girls
        A seer is what England needs
she has been in the hands of
her "history" and her literate
men.
or the grammar school cop-out Wilson
and his Brown ways
a minor Johnson, in other words
a minor nothing, no-
thing is what we have
on both sides, therein does Europe
take pride in the Gaul.
or the hopeless business ventures
of the Italian men and whose fear of hair-cut refusers
like they were major defectors, is theological.
        "I can't get over it,
how extensive the wrong's been—
and how long standing . . . and of course
no fucking *end* in sight: or, which
as you'd know I'd never believe I'd

come to,
        permanently intended disablement"
"the idea that civilization is static.

PART V: WHIT SUNDAY

                    "I la' ta speak the
                    many languages a' English"

England beware
            the cliff of 1945
    turns a natural insularity
    into a late, and out of joint
    naturalism of inbred
    industrial indecision. The hesitation
    to hard sell small arms
    to backward countries and
    "if we must, can't the man
    be more civilized" of a man
    who only knows his business
    be it selling washing machines
    or machine guns: un "produit
    de l'industrie moderne."
                    White Sunday,
    the day of the Big White Sale.
    We speak of payments as
                    balanced
    Oxford, the dull if sometimes
                    remote
            facade
        is balanced in limestone, the
    Bodleian has as a copyright
    every book,
                    Lincoln College
            has high on the wall
            in the first court
        a small bust of John Wesley, fellow
    there is in Merton an Elizabethan

stretch of building and beyond
that, under a passage
the treed lawn where only fellows
and there is the garden where Hopkins
as at Cambridge the tower
where Byron's Bear near
        the rooms of Coleridge
    or Shelley's notebook in the
case at the Bodleian, the Lock
of His Hair, his glove, in a case.
not two gloves as he must
have had two hands to cover
but that hip thing
one glove you can do something
                    with
in terms of those and these brown spectacular
times, two
of course are a boring reminder
we are the animals we are
a lovely glove admittedly
but not so lovely as Shelley.

I walked back from Merton
with two lads who spoke of the police
and their perilous adventures
in Oxford's streets of explanations
"I shall climb up a drain pipe—
"But won't that disturb the authorities?
"it shall disturb them more
"if you wake them to report me
and thus we walked along—
there were more great names
than you'd care to hear
But at one point one of them said
it's impossible to write of it
every substantive fit
to name and celebrate has been spoken
and named. Then there was

a turning, we entered another street which
I'm more used to a grid,
swore to myself I'd never reenter,
but once I loved the idea of such narrow places.
And the easy talk of obscure things
I must admit I envied
                those children
because I love the dazzle of learning
and I am only concerned
when I think the strings
have gone loose.
        if I weren't an intelligent man
I'd share the attitude
        of my president
"Education is a wonderful thing."

                But I said *everything*?
has been talked about
around Oxford. I was assured
it had been. I didn't *say* while walking
but I thought well then make up!
something! Because baby if you don't
they's gonna take all your wine away
they's gonna turn you into a state
institootion and you'll all be working
for the state just like in America
and you'll have to *prove*
you're useful, the most *useless*
sort of proof you'll ever have to make

and once they get the wine off
your table onto *theirs* they're
going to drink that wine just like
Nero always did only Nero
never had the nerve to call it Socialism
and who can blame him: socialism is shit turned only half way round
you better at least start digging up
some hills
to talk about. Get laid, describe that.

the world seems endlessly interested.
Trial title: How I got laid in Oxford without going to Paris or London
Oxford was never intended for defeat
as I understand it it was born
as a dirty necked attempt
to keep clear of the establishment.

"Education's a wonderful thing. Get all
you can get."
Everybody around me
when I was young
said that

The American
who feels the newness of
his continental place, who has been
across the states
and north in Canada or down to Mexico
has been in other words
around his part of the new world
(and it is his part, all Canadians
and Mexicans have one time
or another
been taxi cab drivers in Los Angeles)
he can't ever fight clear
of a mixed truth
he wants to be *good* and greedy simultaneously—
he has been taught the world is ancillary
to us
and only lately
or at least due to recent pressures
in places too boring to name
he has had to decide on false grounds
what he wants to help—the mistake
is inexcusable of course—
but what is unmistakable is
that DeGaulle,
Ho Chi Minn, Chou en-Lai,
LeRoi Jones, Dean Rusk

are all doing the same bit:
pressing
        and they are
all correct—it is their thing
against anybody else's
                    (there is no longer
            any *cause,* the fastest
        with the mostest is the rule
and the trouble with literacy is
        that it enables you to predict
        which side *to be on* which means you are pre-dicted
before anything happens—and
                    if the
            innocent make mistakes
        that's just too bad—
        they either sat around
        or their information was incorrect
and the uninformed always
        trust their paychecks.

                    Thus those children
could start by naming themselves and the rocks
in a larger than
national way and then more intimately,
if only for a more hopeful world
say what hope this "rock
from which the language springs"
can be in the world. Can't
you tell yourselves it is time
Oxford stopped having a place
in English life as sanctuary,
World War II was *not* ended
in Europe because you failed
to take up the language
—not *the* language
oh you still have *that,* you
are stuck with that, that's
all you have,

because you so desired
to be the English Race
you so much wanted the courses
to come in their proper order
"where's the fish" you said
you were so impatient
and now
all you have is a few people you consider
problems anyway who won't even bother to speak
your language
and all they want to do is beat
your unemployment schemes, the best
of them have gone off
to Katmandu, the best of them
aren't even interested, except Tom
      Pickard
    who still makes his own sense
         in Newcastle, but he's a northerner.
    and will steal and resell
every book Calder and Boyars prints
God bless him.

PART VI: OF THE "ENGLISH" COLONIES

No other country
and what others of Europe tried
France, I suppose, still a noxious
excited, unsuccessful
nation
except fanatical spain could
have done it—and she did half.
The Constitution comes from that
its one eye
on property and religion, the twins—envious,
covetous, jealous and mistrustful
timorous, sordid, outwardly dissembling,
sluggish, suspicious, stubborn,
a contemner of women

a close lyar, malicious
murmuring, never contented
ever repining.
Except Spain sent
only the men who were greedy enough
to be trustworthy—the rest of the spanish population
is and was
as inconsequential as Europe's multitudes—
(not you Cabeza)
do you know when western Europe so glibly
      puts down
        America
it puts down, literally,
itself.
do you know *America*
is the world. Think of that.

    To kill it is to want it.
    Every   spade   wants it. wants the shit
       "   chinee   "   "
       "   Pole   "   "
       "   mongoloid   "   "
and   "   mongol   "   "
       "   wop, frog, & spic
    Every Limey wants it
      " swollen bellied, cow loving,
rat worshiping rice eating indian wants it
only he is such a fanatical fink he wants the stinking
DDT infested wheat first
the Corvairs presumably later
which will become "sacred" . . . think of the maintenance bill.

Every obsession-ridden catholic
wants it—he wants the freedom it means to tyrannize
since he has taken food from the most *helpless*
people in the world already

Every communist wants it
since he see a factory already in good shape

Every american also wants it
since he has it and good food is "life" if you don't Bump into
the other carts at the supermarket
not because there is a rush
to cart it away
but because you might have to watch
your neighbors *at it,*
doing it
Eskimoes come down from the north
for it
Doctors cross the *atlantic*
for it—(what they call the "Brain" drain)
Indians (american) migrate
with tickets saying Seattle, Los Angeles,
Tucson, Phoenix, Albuquerque
Cheyenne in their pockets
for it, and when they arrive
they contract TB as if
they had signed beforehand
America has a disease,
good jobs and high pay
and all you have to be
is qualified—get a job?
I get sick myself
sometimes when the people of the world, who have all
gone there, make an
account and the title
is America
and the signatories are
every motherfucker
in the world, only *now*
they think they
            can have the *Idea*
without the thing, they think
it's only a piece of real estate.
                They think they can
distill the poison out
pour it off

213

                    forget
the oldest danger, that to *think*
is to be locked inside the thing. ICE
is what my friend said
we're still in, there are traces
as far south
as brazil. They may think of it as north, there.

America is Everybody's idea:
oppression versus freedom. enthusiastic
advocates for Both persuasions
you'll find from old families
who arrived five minutes ago—
it isn't just the boots and the soggy
crackers who are
                    the increasing
American thing. Somebody used to say
the Jews will be next
but they're even now dated
and replaced by a generation
which is not even Jew but just
that same digit from the rest
                    of the world
filing in to get its concerned throat
cut.
     We have had race
and color and oppression/oppressor
shoved up our asses so long
we don't even see that, *even poets*
   are no longer in communication.
Yevtushenko talking like the chamber of commerce
in Washington
inside the same general language
it is that *bad,* "the many languages
of English"
are as if
they were "foreign," as if commodity
had turned all that sound off, and into
the international times.

Oxford I don't even hate you.
The suggestion of Jude
and that tyranny of facade
to a man who sought
the working out of his sexual place
in the busiest scene
of his time,
                    that the stone *would* not
and *could* not admit him remains just too lamentable. The stone
itself, is common
as america is a creation via common art
will men always be hurled back
until they destroy the stone
itself. That's what
the black men back in my land
propose to do,
tear every
pillar of it
down, and tear the world,
the neat world, down,
It wasn't Jude's thwarted ambition
that's the dullest meanest part
of Hardy's mind, it is the condition
which *permits*
such a hopeless plot we're still stuck with
                                        the new
world was an evil world—
it should never have
been discovered. Columbus
breeds unmentionable
national names they are
indistinguishable from their opportunities.
the mafia are only the tin horns
eager still to be accepted.

We have lived world,
contrary to what you
may think, on the refuse
of what you thought best to send us

                                                    to chooŝe.
(oh my Maryland)   Please
don't send any
        more. The Indians (american) I have their word
for it, are tired of it.

ON THE NATURE OF COMMUNICATION
SEPTEMBER 7, 1966

As Dr. Verwoerd one day
sat at his appointed desk
in the parliament at Capetown
there came to him a green
and black messenger.
(who did not, in fact, disagree with him)

and Dr. Verwoerd looked up
as the appropriately colored man
approached. He expected
a message. What he received
was a message. Nothing else.

That the message was delivered
to his thick neck
and his absolute breast
via a knife
that there was a part tied
to the innate evil of the man
is of no consequence
and as the condolences, irrelevant.

Thus, in the nature of communication
Dr. Robert Kennedy is deeply shocked
and Dr. Wilson shocked

Dr. Portugal, that anonymous transvestite
is "with" the gentle people of
South Africa in this their moment
            of grief
            and wishes them well
in their mischief. A practical
and logical communication. Pope
Johnson also deplored etc.
Dr. Mennen Williams said something about "africa."

By its nature communication
ignores quality and opts for accuracy:
come on, tell us how many nigger's balls
tonight. Do not fold bend spindle or mutilate,
I needn't tell anyone
who has received a paycheck,
is each man's share in the plan.

WAIT BY THE DOOR AWHILE DEATH,
THERE ARE OTHERS

Is this the inch of space in time I have
I awoke just now
I don't know from what
I could suppose a certain gas
                it could have been
        thinking of myself

Is this thing made
with the end built-in
the component of death hidden only
in the youthful machine
but discoverable if the wrench
                of feeling

is turned near forty when the doors
shut with a less smooth click
and biological deliquescence
a tooth broken and unrecoverable
ah news from the Great Manufacturer.

This afternoon someone, an american
from new york, spoke
to me knitting his brows, of
"the american situation" like
wasn't it deplorable, a malignancy
of the vital organs say News
from nowhere. A mahogany sideboard of tastes.
I knitted my brows too
an old response
        and tried to look serious
Look like I was thinking of quote back home.

Look like I *have* a home, pretend
like anyone in the world
I know where that is. And could
if I chose, go there.

I thought sure as hell
he is going down
the whole menu
                        Civil rights cocktail
                        Vietnam the inflexible entree

oh gawd what will there be for pudding
(not another bombe

I shifted deftly out the window
of the new university, the english workers
saunter easily building this thing.

    What has been my stride
My body remains younger
than I am. I let part of my beard grow
in September and touching it

with my hand when I turned in bed
I woke up. Hair on the face is death
it is that repels the people gets
a sociological explanation. Disaffection
is in our day the fear of death
the bare face is thought permanent,
a rock. But not clean.
The cat is cleaner when he licks
his hair and claws following a meal.

I nearly died the other day, without intention.
And when I thought Death had come for me
before My Time I was in a fright
to know what to do last
in what city to meet my gunner Meg
be beside me
                    and laughed
like a tired runner at the end of hurrying.
                    It was dry.
The laughter a hiss at environment.
And just now, reconsidering this
I hear the crows, I have
not seen augurous birds since we moved
away from the rookery in Lexden churchyard
they rise with the dawn now and flutter
in hoarse astonishment
around the top of the sycamore in the garden
the mists from the North Sea move rapidly by.
The wind rushes and turns. "A blackening train
Of clamorous rooks thick urge their weary flight.

I have no more sense of death than
the intimations the starlings
bring and no cold wish to be there
in that place. The rot of finger tips
and an old fern grown full inside my skull
are the passing, dull
presentments I have.
I have felt already the reality

of the last breath I draw in.
I want to say something.
                    I want to talk
turn myself into a tongue

It was a short exhalation
rose from me as the smoke
from a blown out candle
thick with the first vacuum
then suddenly thin, the intention
of a whisper and smile.

The question of the child
"what is it" is only possible
from the neuter distance of the child
when a stranger walks alone
far out on the quay
or, as there are no estuaries
where I come from
across an open field

The crossection of the monument of Death
involves the shadow of
the rushing spider
when it is crushed
but the intersection of the moon
is absolute
    the human presence
        and the power to be
            is that small
        our time and
            place
                is that limited
                    our cry for god
    that weak
        our religion
            that constructed

There was a Saturday gathering
of people
Stones outside shop near Pound's
london residence, Kensington walk
a mews. My dream
had me pound stone. A woman agent
of the university of texas was there
didn't meet her, and another awful creature

from new york.
We drank small glasses of bubbly wine
said to be from Spain, tasting suspiciously
morocco. Headstone.

How we inscribe our days
to boredom. The next week I sat
while a harmless collagist
drew my portrait.
But I was bored past the threat of
Death. It took a double shot of whiskey
in Liverpool street to revive me.

It is difficult enough to sit still for love
and now the price of the time for that
rises like the hem, or goes down
as some predictable opposite. April
is my month. I learn the 6th card
of the major arcana. But so is March
the zodiac cuts me that way, the ram
and the bull, it is love I am
or the 5th, and mediate the material
and divine, a simple sign   the ram
the reflection of Isis. I wear
a tiara. I can think of people
who won't believe that.
                          The body. I am
however, the host of my body.
I invite myself to enter myself.
I have gone there sometimes with great pleasure.

We are not in God's name. At the end,
when the dreaming of the dream
came I "thought" I was Sophia Loren
a mature venus. I don't resemble her.
She could be Mama Courage.

In God's name I do not seek an end.
The imitation of life is more vivid
           than life
                    (Paul, here is your
                    name
                    as cool as anything

So there is a dream story
   of a true enough man named Pedro
"a man without a country"
in the cowering simplicity of the newspaper phrase
it is reported he was a stowaway
on the English cargo ship Oakbank 2 years ago
but he has no papers and every country
rejects him. He says he is Brazilian.
He will ply the seas, a captive there
until he dies. His references do not exist.
No Deans will welcome him. No housewives
have come forth with a cup of coffee
no workers will welcome him upon the job
no greeting of any kind seems forthcoming.
He shall ply the seas until he dies.
His references do not exist. Notice.
No one will recommend him. His first name
is all he has, always the sign of
an acutely luckless man, his first name
can be used by anyone, indeed only
his first name, the excuse for abandoning him
is complete. Even the crew of the Oakbank
I should imagine
are waiting for the day he, idling about the ship
washes over and saves them the handling
of his body against the rail and into the foam

where he at last must be and even now is
as he walks the decks, no nation possesses
the apparatus to fix another identity
or any identity for this man who is without one.
He is the man we all are and yet he doesn't exist.
He is the man we would all save with our tongues
because we are secretly him. His references of course
do not exist. He may recall as we do
the uncertain days on shore
when they did, when once, remember that time
the world seemed open what a satisfying meal
that was. The body outlives
in Pedro too, its lighted parts. The rest
is application, qualified and eager young man
or woman, fluent french and english
would travel . . .

A MORNING TO REMEMBER OR,
E PLURIBUS UNUM

This is a morning to say something.
This is a really keen morning. All over
the world people are gassing
about one thing or another. The globe
which might easily be taken
for a face, or look, Let's call it
the head of a successful novelist
grinning thru space, the plots
I think we can assume
just won't quit. An awful lot
must be happening this morning.

Then there are the little people
inside the Big Novelist, and spinning
on him. They go here and there,
Italy, Spain sometimes but that
doesn't matter, the Big Novelist
keeps an eye on them. This morning
a lot of people started to talk.
A lot of them had some pretty
nasty things to say. Right! they said
Mr. Barber eats Bisto.

                    Ian McIan
likes LBJ with manila icing. But no matter
what people say this morning
the Big Novelist will know about it.
Some people say he squints
when those astronuts and cosmonuts
buzz around his head. The Big Novelist
doesn't like science fiction very much
and if he had fingers, some people think,
he'd pinch them.

(The Adventures, etc. of
    Daddy, the little novelist asked
    the Big Novelist, can I climb on
    your shoulders. No son, Big Novelist said
    it's lonely up here

A NOTATION ON THE EVENING
OF NOVEMBER 27, 1966

The moon is a rough coin tonight
full but screened by lofty moisture
bright enough to make sure
of the addresses
on the letters I drop in the red pillar box
Frost is on the streets. A soft winter breeze
comes from the North Sea into my nostrils
I am at home here only in my mind
that's what heritage is.
Turning the corner, only our windows
along the ribbon of road are lit
I know my wife has gone to bed
and that the gas is burning
and that my heart and my veins
are burning for home. Yet those abrupt times
I hear the harsh voice of home
I am shocked, the hair on my neck
    crawls.
This evening we all went to see
an old classic flick at the Odeon
The magnificent seven introducing
Horst Buchholz, I'd seen it before
and *had not* got it that a german
played a mexican, of course!

An American foreigner is every body
navajoes play iroquois
the American myth is only "mental" a foreigner
is *Anybody*. Theoretically at least
an Italian could play
an English man or a London jew
if nobody knew.
Tom and Jenny were there
and Nick Sedgwick.
Tom remarked, on the evidence of
the last scene when the Mexican-
Japanese said Vaya con Dios
and Yul said a simple adios.
"that was philosophical."
Then the five of us went home
singing Frijoles!
twirling our umbrellas
and walking like wooden legged men in a file
one foot in the gutter
            the other on the sidewalk.

AN IDLE VISITATION

The cautious Gunslinger
of impeccable personal smoothness
and slender leather encased hands
folded casually
to make his knock,
        will show you his map.
There is your domain.
Is it the domicile it looks to be
or simply a retinal block
of seats in, yes of course

226

he will supply the phrase
the theater of impatience.

          If it is all you have,
the footstep in the flat above, in a foreign land
or any shimmer the city
sends you
the prompt sounds
of a metropolitan nearness
          he doesn't have to unroll the map of love.
The knock responds
to its own smile, where
I ask him is my heart
not this pump
artificial already and duty bound
he says, touching me
with his leathern finger
as the queen of hearts burns
from his gauntlet into my eyes.

Globes of fire
he says there will be.
This is for your sadly missing heart
or when two persons meet
it is the grove of Gethsemane
no matter where they are
it is the girl you left
in Juarez, the blank
political days press her now
in the narrow alleys
or in the confines of the river town
her dress is torn
by the misadventure of
          her gothic search
by omission behind carpentered doors
     the mission
bells are ringing in Kansas
Have you left something out?

Negative, says my Gunslinger,
no *thing* is omitted.

I held the reins of his horse
while he went off into the desert
to pee. *Yes,* he sd
when he returned, that's better.
How long, he asked
have you been in this territory.
Four years I sd. Four years.
Then you will no doubt know where we can have
a cold drink before sunset and then a bed
will be my desire if you can find one
for me, I have no wish to continue
my debate with men,
my mare lathers with tedium
her hooves are dry
Look they are covered with the alkali
of the enormous space
between here and formerly.
Need I repeat, we have come
without sleep from Nuevo Laredo

And why do you have a female horse
Gunslinger? I asked. Don't move
he replied
the sun rests deliberately
on the rim of the sierra.

And where will you now I asked.
Five days northeast of here
depending of course on whether one's horse
is of iron or flesh
there is a city called Boston
and in that city there is a hotel
whose second floor has been let
to an inscrutable Texan named Hughes
Howard? I asked
The very same.

And what do you mean by inscrutable,
        oh Gunslinger?
I mean to say that he
has not been seen since 1832.
But when you have found him my Gunslinger
what will you do, oh what will you do?
You would not know
that the souls of old Texans
are in jeopardy in a way not common
to other men, young man.

You would not know
of the long plains night
where they carry on
and arrange their genetic duels
with men of other states—
so there is a longhorn bull half mad
half deity
who awaits an account from me
back of the sun you nearly disturbed
just then. Here hold my mare
I must visit the cactus once more
and then, we'll have that drink.

SONG

Again, I am made the occurrence
Of one of her charms. Let me
Explain. An occupier
Of one of the waves of her intensity.

                  One meeting

Behind the back
      of the world
Brief and fresh
And then
Nothing.
Winter nights
The crush of fine snow
A brilliancy of buildings around us
Brief warmth
In the cold air, the cold temperament
Of a place I can't name

        Now what is it. Turning into
A shadowed corridor half the earth away
And deep inside an alien winter
I remember her laugh
The strange half step she took

            And I would not believe it
If Europe or England
Could in any sense evoke her without *me,*
The guitar of her presence the bearer of her scent
Upon my wrist
The banding of her slightsmiling lassitude . . .

THE SUNDERING U.P. TRACKS

(the end of the North Atlantic Turbine poem

I never hear the Supremes
but what I remember Leroy.
McLucas came
to Pocatello the summer of 1965
one dark night he was there
in a brilliant white shirt, one
dark evening the U.P.
brought him, the most widely luminous
and enchorial smile
        I ever saw.
                He had taken rooms
with the Reverend Buchanan
over in that part of town owned
by Bistline, the famous exploiter.

I was hurt to discover he had come
to what I thought was my town in my fair country
three days before. I had thought
he would stay with me.
How many thousand years too late now
is that desire. How long will the urge to be
remain. Every little bogus town
on the Union Pacific bears the scar
of an expert linear division.

                The rustic spades
                at the Jim Dandy Club
                took his money
                like sea winds lift
                the feathers of a gull

      "Compared to the majestic legal thievery
of Commodore Vanderbilt men like Jay Gould
and Jim Fisk were second-story workers . . ."

(rest comfortably Daniel Drew)

Each side of the shining double knife
from Chicago to Frisco
to Denver, the Cheyenne cutoff
the Right of Way they called it
and still it runs that way
right through the heart
the Union Pacific rails run also to Portland.
Even through the heart of the blue beech
hard as it is.

                    2000 miles or so
                each hamlet
              the winter sanctuary
                    of the rare Jailbird
              and the Ishmaelite
              the esoteric summer firebombs
          of Chicago
                the same scar tissue
                I saw in Pocatello
          made
          by the rapacious geo-economic
          surgery of Harriman, the old isolator
          that ambassador-at-large

You talk of color?
Oh cosmological america, how well
and with what geometry
you teach your citizens

THE COSMOLOGY OF FINDING YOUR PLACE

The *Resistantism* of all other places
On the floor among filters and the Spillings
   The cosmology of the floor of the Nation
   The cosmology of finding your place
     The cosmology of smelling and feeling your Natural place
     inside the place, feeling the filters
       feeling the rock, feeling the roll
       feeling the social spray at that level
         low down, with the filters and the feet
         feeling the place you can fold all four legs
         and be man's best friend to the End, among the filters
         and the feet, in the rock, and in the roll
         in the clock and in the roll, in the hole
         of the social bilge **The Great White Dog**
      of the Rockchalk, seeks his place Seeks
       The place for Him there, tries every scrap of Space
     The Great White Dog of The Rockchalk Cafe
     moves under the Social seeking his own Place
   in the constant present snap of eternity
   listening with the german dislocated castenet
  His Nose Is under the great pin ball rolling in heaven above
  thru the barren terrain of feet He moves
from place to place seeking his place
The resisters the dogs seek their place
WAYNE KIMBALL told me all this
WAYNE KIMBALL sits in the booths, *WAYNE KIMBALL*
knows about the *Great White Dog of the Rockchalk*
The Great White Dog of The Rockchalk doesn't
 The Great White Dog has been there
Western Civilization is Beer
  The Great White Dog of The Rockchalk
  went thru the door of Western Civilization
   Which is north of the Barbershop
   and north of the sailor pants incense shop
    The Great White Dog went between all that

and the Gaslight, *The Great White Rockchalk dog*
shakes hands with both paws indiscriminately
For he Seeks his own true place on the floor
He disregards the social He seeks the Place
he seeks The Space his **soul** can occupy
In His restless search he looks only for the Place
Where he can come to rest in his own true Place
and that might be on the floor of the rockchalk
The great *White Dog* is not Interdicted by opinion
He accepts the floor of the *Rock Chalk* as an Area,
like any other, he will test that space
He is preoccupied only with the Search
The Great White dog of the Rockchalk is not social
WAYNE KIMBALL told me all this, *WAYNE KIMBALL*
is social, he knows only persons, he doesn't
give a shit for the floor of the *Rockchalk*
WAYNE KIMBALL is neurotic like us, he wants
to smoke Grass, *WAYNE KIMBALL* sits in the booths
WAYNE KIMBALL drinks beer, has a part time job
pretending to be literate, *WAYNE KIMBALL* uses
the telephone and all other public Utilities
including Cocaine, *The Great White Dog*
of the Rock Chalk is full of shit and can't shit
until he finds his place, *WAYNE KIMBALL* has diarrhea
WAYNE KIMBALL hasn't got a driver's license
WAYNE KIMBALL is thin and knows everything that happens
He has ears, He is a corrupt little mongrel like us
turned on to everything hopeless and bullshit
The Great White Dog of The Rockchalk is dumb
and doesn't know anything but his instinct for the search
for his place somewhere in the litter
of the filters and the literally dropped dreams
of the *Great Rock Chalk,* he smells the dreams
on the floor dropped from between the legs
of young English majors, ejected from between the
Dual Spraycans of the fraternizers
He seeks his place on top of this matter
among the feet of the privileged nation on the floor

of the *Great shit, Rock Chalk Rock Chalk White Rock
Chalk Dog, And* WAYNE KIMBALL Smokes cigarettes
and Thoreaus them ontoOntoOntoOnto the floor
already predicated by cancer, the slow movement of *Cancer*
and I love these dogs because they are us and more us
than we are and they seek their places as do the true
whether they are *Resisters* or just scared or both
They are the twin dogs of creation in our image
and I give them both the floor as I give the *Resisters*
This Poem from the throne of Belief as the **Egyptians**
Gave and took from the Dogs Their access to Heaven
That we may all be Gods and seek our Place.

[presented april 10, 1969 at the united campus
christian fellowship benefit reading for the
draft resisters league, Lawrence]

LOVE SONGS

1

It is deep going from here
from the old world to the new
from Europa home
the brilliant scrolls of the waves
                    wave
the runic secret of homeward
when Diego de Landa
the glyphic books destroyed
there were old towns
            in our hemisphere sadness
now as then

no sense in old towns chontal
                    got to have
newtowns of the soul

2

Inside the late nights of last week
under the cover of our selves
you went to sleep in my arms
and last night too

you were in some alarm
of your dream
                    some tableau
an assembling of signs
from your troubled day glows
and trembles, your limbs
divine with sleep
gather and extend their flesh
along mine
and this I surround, all this
I had my arms around

3

My speech is tinged
my tongue has taken
a foreigner into it
Can you understand
my uncertainties grow
and underbrush and thicket
of furious sensibility
between us and wholly
unlike the marvelously burning
bush which lies at the entrance
to your gated thighs

My dear love, when I unsheathe
a word of the wrong temper
it is to test that steel
across the plain between us

4

Or if the word falls—
   but I didn't *mean* that
too often and too soon
before it moves
carried in our mouths
into the bright orchard
of a desire we must build traps
to catch
so that we are free
we think, to answer all
who would delay us,
it is our *selves* dressed
as the clothed figures who beseech us
for Our lives to beware
destruction, *take care* is
the password to their stability

5

Carried in our mouths
the warm sperm rises
and prolongs us—as we are
everyway locked
inside the warm halls of flesh
which is in our kind
filled by a song for all lovers—
How are you? is simply
another transcendental question

I'd know you were my katalysis
had we never met, in all space
I am fixed beyond you, the cruel
is a decision of the stars, in all space
our clef is pitched together
we share
a completely trued voice
our substance carried
in our joined mouths
flows

6

The cleft in our ages
is an echoing cañon—look
I insist on my voice
Archeus become my life
and as any other extension
not to be ignored—
if you were my own time's possession
I'd tell you to *fuck off*
with such vivid penetration
you'd never stop gasping
and pleasure unflawed
would light our lives, pleasure
unrung by the secretly expected
fingers of last sunday

Do you hear me, can you
please only agree with me
because poems and love
and all that happens in the street
are blown forward
on the lightest breeze

7

But you are a green plant to me
only to be acknowledged
with passion
tended by my whole attention
there is argument only in equality
one war we can hope to ignore

What we have done is embroidered
our two figures are
as if set forth from Bayeux
and I fly like a dragon standard
yet my soul because I left home
as you did
pulls against a martingale
and having stayed at home too
or more
how much more pulls against you

8

Now the scorpion
crawls on my shoulder
and bold as the quartered arrow
of Mars though I am
beat down, too
under the drag of what
we conjure with what
choosing among the real
with the accuracy of image
we see
the problematic figure of youth
across the Atlantic
of a past love, or passed?
and there he is, reconstituted
water dressed in a freer present
than any present past
and your eyes tonight are journals
of unburnt records

9

EYE high gloria
    a fine europ ean morn ing
    black coffee
for Nick in the nick of time
he gives me something for you
and Otis Redd ing
with his feet up watching
infinity roll in and Nick
his time ing
and sudden lee the lid
comes off
        and we head straight for
the thing we could be in
cannabic warm
and rime ing

10

Who could have told me love
is always love
and all it's needs to be
where it needs to be
are you
I thought forgive me
it was something you do
now everywhere I turn
and everytime there is
that full thing with us
I am cottered
        high inside you
   lutus

11

You are not easy to enter

      Omega

you are a double letter
and I am equal only
     to my own singularity

the mixed strings of aries begins
you are sometimes in the trance of what
is beyond you,

         sometimes close
and then you turn into it
     so fast we turn

into another room we hear inside
and all the people looking
over the wall
are frozen

12

      Not this
not that
  and not this nor
    not this or that
    nor caught
on poles at
   all I have
          no place
outside might welcome
might warm me

  I am nothing
anymore at all
than in myself, you be
a still center
which has about it pivoting
ramifications of my strain
a marvellously pure crystal
the center still and in me
        located
and in the ten thousand
years or more
     will change
  and be
  the shift, location
and polaris
   a new name

13

I feel that fear
    my own
that fear a face presents
    and looks
and says words and the words
mean something
        else
and the fear
is inside the other meaning

       meaning which

would have no meaning then
of the thing that's not itself
would fear not itself
        fear not,

could have no meaning
Don't kill me
with that other meaning

14

The largest center we know
makes his move
sundown in the window
and in space, double space
each one a concentration of
the other a difficult fact to absorb
it is a double labor to love
one twin
and Nájera crosses my table
praising the audacity of an early death
Do you know where we are now
we have come here the day after
the announcement
      and we look at our lives
      in a camera

We made the journey by train
it was cold now and then
a day scored by a cloud
the heat we had we had in our pockets
and occasionally we took some
what more can be said
more than the existence we have

15

The question is not to you, you know
the indisputability of the soul
do you know where we are now
do you know the platform any more than
I arrived at the same time one september
what was crossed
is still crossed
and the agent's dark eyes
burn from the dark short past
represent, handles the claims
of those we over ran
and they scream with their
fixed smiles
for satisfaction
do you know where we are now
from my soul I want to know
from my beginning in and out
within me
and now returned home
from somewhere abroad
on the second day of april
with the snow

16

When the duel

        the split
the collateral
of the mirror
the sisters
in the scrolls of foam
the trans parency
of the mirror
        in that lure
you say goodbye
you say hello
reflected, and see this—
your personality, as such
would be complicated
even if you had been

        born all by yourself

17

The imagined
      is the quality of life Paris
not the bones in the fish
in the oppression
of La Coupole, the drama of
our time, masks, a dramatic
event dinner, turns, grin
frown, tables
a view of that world
open and filled
with the prospect, the long
perspective of the pain
of my life
in that text

18

    The Steppes
on the Plains
were the two maps
we joined, our lives
as two complex areas
a marriage
we'll never have to prove

19

My solid energy state breeds
extreme movement in juxt
aposed blocks of space

      Hermes standing

anyone from the beginning of time
will know the initiation of time
covered with sperm

20

21

She will permit
any property of herself
any slanted permission
but make you know
any property is a careful
waste of time

Thus it was revealed
the bed was covered by a skin
brought away from Delphi

22

The agony is beauty
that you can't have that
and sense too. There
is no sense to beauty. It offends
everyone, the more so
in ratio to the praise of it.
And I've known this for a long
time, there has been no
great necessity to say it. How
really, the world is shit
and I mean all of it

23

And then, if you come
to the mountains, what
is there more, ore in mines
ore in veins, or more fully than
you might have had it elsewhere
Call them the Rockie mountains.
There is a vast smell of marriage
not lightly said, some place
some time ago I was there too.

I've been everywhere.
This afternoon I thought why not,
why not get Jenny into something
and we both fly off to meet,
well, almost anyone. Away
from the flat rancorous smell
of their insinuation, which is
just this: you've done the thing—
you've presumed your body
as well as your mind, *your mind*
we like to watch go through its sideshow
lifted up in the bright creative air
but when you made other arrangements
for your body, baby go away, that's it

24

There is no final word
for how you are.
An emotional response
can be the reputation to
which all inquiry is referred
and let go at that.

Back Home, Back Home
the day wakes up and once
out the door into what's
left of the fresh air it still
comes clear
how lovely
love is there

SONGS: SET TWO: A SHORT COUNT

1

The resin of the Pine
white cast in amber
planted and watered
in the river of the blood
across the bench
of the mountain
in the full mirage of the world
grove where the gnosis
lets go into hold of creation

2

3

We doné the crossing of the border
In the lysergium of September
With the aid of two camerados
We won that entry again
Between the pulse of the World Breath
Through the desire for symmetry, the plane
On which we go and come
Oh my darling kid my darling thing
My darling twin
And your offspring
From out of the dark hall we came

4

Within the animation of the universe
blood draws back
into the interior
when we breathe in
and rushes out when
we breathe out, out of the body
Love pours back
                    like Mach
                    the world breath

5

The Kid on the Ute board
of a Colorado woman,
the core of Vulcan on
the horizon
a member of Earth is god
these are members of Earth
cast from womans thigh
stringing spiral cord

6

Soft flex
by the blood between you filled
the brilliance of the lysergium
burning in the animal birth
a message from the unrelenting
center of the sun itself rolling
on the edge of heaven O
cut my darling away from him let the resin
kneed with the world breath

7

Barrier, great Barrier
and inventory, system of
the nation's soul
Barrier of its fat
point-blank intuition.
Apply the metaphor
the fabric woven or go as you are
acid of the marvellous detail
of your skin, tapestry
of creation, your passport
was not made to reflect such a vision

8

The numberless equals
seek to impose a grinning punishment
the frieze of grinning monsters
hysterically normal hung from the arm
of their dispositions stuffed
inside fixed up unable to carry
the heavy thing away from your
big wonderful splendor

9

Board the ship
You are are you not
The ship
Your quivering vessel
Center of the thing
Lysania, viscount
In whose simple gut
Are fixed seats for
The simple minority
A ship which psychic tensors
From burning foreheads
Emit move roar
With laughter noblesse
And monstrousness, moves
From these unwilling communards

The power comes unabated comes
Swifter
Until velocity rules
And the supplicants of
Their own arrival twist
Under the influence
Of Pluto
Their cheeks lay writhe
Paper thin against
                    their cheekmounds
The fat melts
And fries their tongues
With what they say
                  What they say

10

Are carnate from it
Popped out
A cargo of unblessed idiots
Fly over the ironic Ocean

11

When I look at you
you're on, the most super
officially we're a gross
very carefully packed
But the most super
Immigrants who bring
Their dumb state
Into the new world
The result of big preparation
So smile like you meant it

12

Are you talking
About the absolute zero
To which you go
You are the basket
In which lie
Your questions. Is a man
Without quest
A dangerous sign

13

14

Give Up your vain lateral borders
Empedocles sphere is
a power of time
the borders of receding time
our breath is not the time, leaves
blown in the world wind
the goat, and flanked
in the night sky
by the horses their brilliance
without end

14

Seen in the light cone
space is a factor of God
and will merely increase
mirrored aspects of anything
not just reality
or theory, Strife is process
(O'Brien
              Any moment
Any place, throughout movement
which no movement is relevant
Love moves
              Bones were one
animal parts formed under Love
wandered about
desiring flesh to become Monsters
harmonious creatures of no distinction of sex

              With equal shares of fire and water
an advance upon separate limbs which
were created by Love and belong then
from Love's point of view
to a world where Love's power
is increasing
              so predominance

is the sign of Strife's power
Our World
is the news of Strife's wandering

      Whole
natured forms, the arrogance
of self-sufficiency, torn men are
and women an expression
and so short lived apparently

      to be unable
to get back even as far as the present
and those monsters who display
the unseparated limbs of Love

15

Pluralities are on the increase
the hunt is on, galaxia
turn with the blood, blood
and strife will not be manipulated
touch not these cells,
come back now, unmolested guardian
thru the various world the battleground
outrage belongs to the virus their pragma
is a cold one, their attention was attracted

16

Then there is dry love
on the dying vessel
the sweet alcohol of the skin
the sweet body
rubbed with love whispers
over the tongue is spread
a desert and this
is the wilderness

17

Intuition is nothing
Intuition is yourself
Your Self

18

Common tongue of the world
scarlet from the head of a man

19

Come to know
The white field falling from the house
Where afternoon runs into the Sun
The snowe filled field
Beneath it
The red floor of ice
A blue space to keep it in
His Newengland

THE KULTURAL EXCHANGE

"Nobody loves me but my mother
And she could be jivin too"
—b. b. king

Slinger, an idle question the poet asked
Are you considered a learned man?

Perhaps

What haps?

You meant whose

I can't choose

  I can follow that lapse
so I shall reveal to you
what I know via Information
I c'gnitioned long ago
that whatever is put in
is triggered with impurity
and however entertaining that might be
it is killing you
with the clicking routine of a rosary
therefore if there is anything to know
I shut mine eyes
on a count of three seconds
and if I get the bit thats it
and if not I have another go

What information do you have
from this process?
Practically none
just one in fact
There is a saying
they have on Mars
  "Sonne in the blue sky zero degrees
  like the first polkadot"

258

"Far Out,"
so you know
practically nothing

Thats correct, nothin
I'm almost
pure Exformation

Anyway, the poet urged
try a 3 second bit
and see what you get

OK the Slinger breathed
He shut his lids
and 3 seconds passed
Behind Them

What! the poet whispered

A fat man with white hair
under a blue baseball cap
and a green shirt
under babyblue bib overalls

What are his feet in?

Didn't get his feet.

You mean you didn't get the whole bit?

We rarely do, You
tell me what he had his feet in

It wasnt my bit

But Exformation is common
youve seen this outcrop
a dozen times
one place or another, dont be confused
because it comes from *My* head
Now, without trying
tell me what the bits feet were in

Uh, Shoes, the poet hesitated

The Slinger crossed his lids
to rerun the three second bit
A-minus, he whispered

Whats that for the poet enquired

     A-minus is your grade
it indicates youre slightly tired
it's like a desperately correct answer
yor imagination was fard
with a Tom Sawyer Programme
a soft con to paint the fence
Id suggest you learn to think
with a touch of sense

then you can use yor head
as an Intake for solid liquid & gas
which Must be Why
He ran a line clear down to your ass

Gee, that blows me out,
I hadnt felt it like that Master
but now I can see your process is faster
and it's quite suddenly discrete
that his feet were *in his feet*

Im proud of you,
the Slinger beamed . . .

[Chicago Day 113]

HEAVY ACQUISITION

The Hamadryas Baboon at the Lincoln Park Zoo
Has gone crazy
In the Silence beyond the glass boundary he bangs
His head
And under his elegant shouldercloak he bites
His foot
Now he is still, considering the wall from the porch
Of his eyes

The Hamadryas is a sacred Egyptian
These keepers have Fury locked up here

[Autumn 1971]

EASY'S BEST

a big Silver belt for Sal

Easy to get up in the mornin
With the soft world
And wonder why we keep the G
On everything back north

Easy 8th street
Easy drift on Magazine street
In the lazy Javelin
Easy to see those very trashy Dragons
          Really Easy

Very easy to wear the flowers
Easy to love, I imagine

261

And if anybody didn't think
And just went down they'd find it
Easy to see N'awlins in the mawnin.

THE POET LETS HIS

TONGUE HANG DOWN

I would Enquire of you
The Slinger leaning forward askt
One of the 4 Great Questions
Least troubling my mind since my arrival:

WHO ARE THE BARBARIANS?

    As if in a space elapsed
between our sighting then hearing a jet
The Poet grew pale
and his blazering transister fell
from his Ivory Fingers
       four of whom
       jumped off at the knuckles
       and ran off with all his rings
       and straightaway sent notes
       to the six who stayed
       expressing contempt and dismay

And the temperature fell in his veins
and his mouth weakened
and grew slack
and his eye left the track
and wandered about the landscape
unlocused and his tongue
fell out over his chin

and his nose migrated
even as Gondwana too gorged
on the immensities of time to be observed
so that its movement must be proven
by the striations of its slippage
as they are the Scars of the Earth
And his ears floated upward
as if Helium was all they heard
and his feet come off and sped over the horizon
leaving the wings of his ankles behind
    and his shoes filled with dust
    an instant ghost town complete
    with banging shutters and peeling posters
    Announcing the stark Indifferentist proposition
        DEAD or ALIVE
    when behold! the galloping Cosmographer
    dropped under his mount
    and blew out the OR

Then his hair fell away
in a dust bowl condition
Like in the Grapes of Wrath
and things come to that
all the people of his barren scalp
packed up and found their way to California
around the craters in this once rich terrain,
the High Planes we shall call them

And his brain snapped shut like a greasy spoon
When the last customer has et his chops
    then gone out the door wiping his chin
    with one hand While the other buys The Times
    which he reads standing on the corner
    toothpick in his mouth *Rams Clobber Lions*
    in his eye
    and turns the pages to the comics where Rex Morgan
    is performing and can't be reached
    as his hand comes up from scratching his ass
    to catch the pages in the Michigan Winde

But the poet's Head was during this lapse
busy with alterations
and when the job was done
the bang of hammers
the whine of bandsaws gone
And all the baffling pulled off
his Head was a pyramid
the minimum solid

And his eyes came home
trying to look like the trip had been a bore
when signs to the contrary
were all over the floor

And he smiled
But the eye atop his pyramid
Would say no more

EXECUTIONER, STAY THY COLD BLADE

As knowledge grows
it becomes apparent
that the brain
is a machine
of a type
very different
from those made hitherto
by the thotfull
    efforts of man

Its success is largely due
to the richness
of its parallel circuits
and its redundancies

This makes it very difficult
to assign particular functions,
especially
by the technique of removal

THE OCTOPUS THINKS WITH ITS ARMS

Out of the total of some 500 million nerve-cells
300 million and more are in the arms

The script in the memory
does not include the recognition of oblique rectangles

In the optic lobes of an octopus
we meet the first great sections of the visual computing system
a Mass of 50 million neurons behind each eye

The optic lobes themselves can be regarded as the classifying
and encoding system and as the Seat of the Memory

The male Octopus Vulgaris fucks by putting the tip
of his third arm
inside the mantle of the female
who sits several feet away
looking like Nothings Happening for about a half hour

The females are impregnated before they are mature
the spermatophores survive until the eggs are ripe
Both animals are covered with vertical stripes during their session
and move not at all.

THE HISTORY OF FUTURES

The long horn was an automotive
package of hide & bones, a few hundred
pounds of dope which delivered itself
entirely free of moral inconvenience
known otherwise as fat
yet with a memory fresh enough to market

The Bloody Red Meat Habit
dates from about 1870
Before that we were a Sowbelly Nation
feeding off the wisest of the omnivores
Beef is the earliest element
of the crisis, a typical texas imbalance

Importations, trash beef from Argentina
are meant to satisfy
the Bloody Red Meat Habits
of our best friends, and in fact
as pet lovers secretly understand
you Can fool fido

With Foodstamps we have pure script
the agricultural subsidy farmers have enjoyed
under every name but socialismo
since World War II

Which brings us
to a truly giant dog named Ronald
the most immense friend conceivable
a Fenrir created by beef heat
and there you have your bullshit apocalysis

One morning, in his mythological greed
He swallows the Sunne

[for my students at Kent State
Spring, 1973]

266

THE STRIPPING OF THE RIVER

The continental tree supports the margins
In return for involuntary atrophos
Which can now be called the Shale Contract
Not only are the obvious labors
In metal and grain and fuel extracted
But the spiritual genius is so apt
To be cloven from this plain of our green heart
And to migrate to the neutralized
And individualizing conditions of the coasts
That this center of our true richness
Also goes there to aberrant rest
Bought by the silver of sunrise
And the gold of sunset.

INDEX OF TITLES AND FIRST LINES

*Titles of poems are
given in italics*